Financial Freedom Formula

Strategies to Build Wealth and Live Debt-Free and Your Pathway to Wealth and Financial Security

By Roger E. Wolfe

Copyright © 2024 by Roger E. Wolfe

All rights reserved. No part of this book may be reproduced, distributed, or transmitted in any form or by any means, including photocopying, recording, or other electronic or mechanical methods, without the prior written permission of the publisher, except in the case of brief quotations embodied in critical reviews and certain other noncommercial uses permitted by copyright law. For permission requests, write to the publisher, addressed "Attention: Permissions Coordinator," at the address below.

Table of Contents

Introduction to Financial Freedom Formula

Chapter 1: Setting the Foundation

Chapter 2: Building a Strong Financial Base

Chapter 3: Maximizing Income

Chapter 4: Mastering the Art of Saving

Chapter 5: Investing for the Future

Chapter 6: Protecting Your Wealth

Chapter 7: Achieving Financial Independence

Chapter 8: Overcoming Obstacles

Conclusion

Introduction to Financial Freedom Formula

Understanding Financial Freedom

Financial freedom is a term that has gained significant attention in recent years, especially as people seek ways to break free from the constraints of traditional employment and pursue lives that align more closely with their personal values and passions. But what exactly does financial freedom mean, and why is it so important in today's world? This section will explore these questions in depth, as well as address common misconceptions that often cloud the understanding of what it truly means to be financially free.

What is Financial Freedom?

At its core, financial freedom refers to a state where an individual has enough wealth to live comfortably without having to work actively for their income. It means having sufficient savings, investments, and cash flow to afford the lifestyle you want for yourself and your family, without being bound to a 9to5 job or relying on a paycheck from an employer. Financial freedom is not just about being rich; it's about having control over your finances and, by extension, your life.

Achieving financial freedom means different things to different people. For some, it might mean the ability to retire early and travel the world. For others, it might mean the security of knowing they can handle emergencies without going into debt or the freedom to choose work based on passion rather than necessity. It's a deeply personal concept, and one's definition of financial freedom can evolve over time as life circumstances change.

Financial freedom is not necessarily synonymous with wealth or having a high income. While earning more can certainly contribute to financial freedom, it is not the only factor. The key to financial freedom lies in how well you manage your money, how much you save and invest, and the financial decisions you make along the way. A person with a modest income but disciplined saving and investing habits may achieve financial freedom faster than someone with a high income but poor financial management skills.

The Importance of Financial Freedom in Modern Life

In today's fast paced and often unpredictable world, financial freedom has become more important than ever. The traditional model of working for 40 years, saving a portion of your salary, and then retiring on a pension is increasingly becoming outdated. Economic changes, shifts in job markets, and the rising cost of living mean that many people need to take a more proactive approach to securing their financial futures.

One of the most compelling reasons to strive for financial freedom is the sense of security it provides. When you are financially free, you are less vulnerable to unexpected life events, such as job loss, illness, or economic downturns. You have the financial cushion to weather these storms without the stress that comes from living paycheck to paycheck. This financial security allows you to make decisions based on what is best for you and your family, rather than what is necessary to keep the bills paid.

Financial freedom also brings a significant amount of personal freedom.

When you are not dependent on a paycheck to cover your basic needs, you have the luxury to pursue your passions, hobbies, and interests. You can choose to work on projects that are meaningful to you, spend more time with family and friends, or even dedicate time to volunteer work. The ability to structure your life around your values and desires, rather than financial necessity, is a powerful motivator for many people seeking financial freedom.

In addition to personal and financial security, financial freedom can lead to better mental and emotional wellbeing.

Financial stress is a significant source of anxiety and tension for many people. The constant worry about paying bills, managing debt, and saving for the future can take a toll on your mental health. Achieving financial freedom can alleviate this stress, leading to a more balanced and fulfilling life.

Furthermore, financial freedom is essential for planning and achieving long term goals. Whether it's buying a home, starting a business, funding your children's education, or planning for retirement, having control over your finances gives you the ability to plan effectively and make informed decisions. It allows you to allocate resources to your priorities and work towards achieving your life goals without being hindered by financial constraints.

Common Misconceptions About Financial Freedom

While financial freedom is a desirable goal for many, there are several misconceptions that can derail efforts to achieve it. Understanding and addressing these misconceptions is crucial for anyone on the path to financial independence.

1. Financial Freedom Equals Being Rich

One of the most common misconceptions is that financial freedom is synonymous with being rich. While wealth can certainly contribute to financial freedom, they are not the same thing. Financial freedom is more about having enough resources to live the life you want without financial stress, rather than accumulating vast amounts of money. A person can be financially free without being wealthy, as long as their income, savings, and investments are sufficient to meet their needs and goals.

2. You Need a High Income to Achieve Financial Freedom

Another misconception is that only those with high incomes can achieve financial freedom. While a higher income can make it easier to save and invest, it is not a prerequisite for financial freedom. Many people with average or even modest incomes have achieved financial freedom through disciplined saving, smart investing, and living below their means. The key is to manage your money wisely, regardless of your income level.

3. Financial Freedom is Only for Older People

Some people believe that financial freedom is something that can only be achieved later in life, after decades of hard work and saving. However, financial freedom is not agespecific. With careful planning and disciplined financial habits, it is possible to achieve financial freedom at any stage of life. In fact, many young people are now pursuing financial independence early in their careers, allowing them to retire in their 30s or 40s if they choose.

4. Financial Freedom Means Never Working Again

Another misconception is that financial freedom means never having to work again. While some people may choose to stop working once they achieve financial freedom, others may continue to work, but on their own terms. Financial freedom gives you the flexibility to choose how you spend your time, whether that means working parttime, pursuing a passion project, or starting a business. The key difference is that work becomes a choice, not a necessity.

5. You Need to Sacrifice Enjoyment to Achieve Financial Freedom

Many people believe that in order to achieve financial freedom, they must live a life of extreme frugality, sacrificing all enjoyment and pleasure. While it's true that financial freedom requires discipline and smart financial choices, it doesn't mean you have to deprive yourself of all the things you enjoy. The goal is to find a balance between enjoying life today and planning for the future. By prioritizing your spending and making intentional choices, you can enjoy your life while still working towards financial freedom.

6. Financial Freedom is a One Time Achievement

Some people think of financial freedom as a destination that you reach and then never have to think about again. In reality, financial freedom is an ongoing process that requires regular monitoring and adjustment. As life circumstances change, your financial goals and strategies may need to evolve as well. Achieving financial freedom is a significant milestone, but maintaining it requires continued attention to your finances and lifestyle choices.

7. Financial Freedom is Impossible for People with Debt

Debt can feel like a significant obstacle to financial freedom, but it doesn't have to be a permanent barrier. With the right strategies, such as debt consolidation, budgeting, and disciplined repayment, it is possible to pay off debt and work towards financial freedom. In fact, many people who have achieved financial freedom started with significant debt but were able to overcome it through careful planning and perseverance.

8. Financial Freedom Requires Complex Financial Knowledge

Another misconception is that achieving financial freedom requires a deep understanding of complex financial instruments and strategies. While knowledge of personal finance is certainly helpful, you don't need to be a financial expert to achieve financial freedom. The basic principles of saving, investing, and living within your means are accessible to everyone. With a commitment to learning and applying these principles, anyone can work towards financial freedom.

9. Financial Freedom is Only About Money

Finally, it's important to recognize that financial freedom is not just about money. While having enough financial resources is a key component, financial freedom is also about the lifestyle and choices that those resources enable. It's about having the freedom to spend your time in ways that are meaningful to you, whether that means traveling, pursuing hobbies, spending time with loved ones, or contributing to causes you care about. Financial freedom is ultimately about living a life that is true to your values and goals, free from the constraints of financial worry.

Chapter 1

Setting the Foundation

Achieving financial freedom is not merely a matter of crunching numbers or following strict budgets. While these elements are certainly important, the journey toward financial independence begins in the mind. The mindset you cultivate, the beliefs you hold, and the goals you set will lay the foundation for your financial success. In this chapter, we will explore the importance of developing a wealth mindset, overcoming limiting beliefs, cultivating an abundance mentality, and understanding the psychology of money. Additionally, we will discuss how to define your financial goals, set SMART objectives, differentiate between short term and long term goals, and understand the importance of vision and purpose in your financial journey.

The Mindset of Wealth

The first step in achieving financial freedom is to adopt the mindset of wealth. This involves shifting your thinking from a scarcity mentality—where you believe that resources are limited and that money is hard to come by—to a mindset of abundance, where you see opportunities for growth and prosperity everywhere. The mindset of wealth is about believing that you have the power to create and attract wealth, and that financial success is within your reach.

One of the key aspects of the wealth mindset is taking responsibility for your financial life. People with a wealthy mindset understand that their financial situation is the result of their choices, actions, and attitudes. They do not blame external circumstances or other people for their financial challenges. Instead, they take ownership of their financial decisions and are proactive in seeking ways to improve their financial situation.

Another important aspect of the wealth mindset is the belief in continuous learning and personal growth. Financially successful people understand that building wealth requires knowledge and skills, and they are committed to lifelong learning. They seek out information, education, and experiences that will help them grow their wealth and manage their finances more effectively. Whether it's reading books on personal finance, attending seminars, or learning from mentors, those with a wealthy mindset are always looking for ways to improve their financial acumen.

Finally, the wealth mindset is characterized by a focus on long term thinking. People with a wealth mindset understand that building wealth takes time, and they are willing to delay gratification and make sacrifices in the short term for greater rewards in the future. They are patient, disciplined, and committed to their long term financial goals.

Overcoming Limiting Beliefs

Limiting beliefs are negative thoughts or attitudes that hold you back from achieving your full potential. When it comes to money, limiting beliefs can be particularly damaging because they can prevent you from taking the actions necessary to build wealth. Common limiting beliefs around money include thoughts like "I'll never be rich," "Money is the root of all evil," or "I'm just not good with money."

To overcome limiting beliefs, the first step is to identify them. Pay attention to the thoughts and attitudes you have about money. Are there certain negative beliefs that keep coming up? Do you feel a sense of anxiety or discomfort when thinking about money? Once you have identified your limiting beliefs, the next step is to challenge them. Ask yourself whether these beliefs are really true, or if they are simply assumptions you have made based on past experiences or societal conditioning.

For example, if you believe that "I'll never be rich," challenge that belief by asking yourself what evidence you have to support it. Are there people who have come from similar backgrounds or faced similar challenges who have achieved financial success? What steps can you take to change your financial situation? By questioning and challenging your limiting beliefs, you can begin to replace them with more empowering thoughts.

In addition to challenging your limiting beliefs, it's important to surround yourself with positive influences. The people you spend time with can have a significant impact on your mindset. If you are surrounded by people who have a scarcity mentality and negative attitudes toward money, it can be difficult to overcome your own limiting beliefs. Seek out individuals who have a positive relationship with money, who are financially successful, and who can inspire and motivate you to achieve your financial goals.

Finally, practice positive affirmations to reinforce your new beliefs. Positive affirmations are statements that you repeat to yourself to help shift your mindset. For example, you might say, "I am capable of building wealth," or "Money flows easily and abundantly into my life." By consistently repeating these affirmations, you can reprogram your mind to believe in your ability to achieve financial success.

Cultivating an Abundance Mentality

An abundance mentality is the belief that there are enough resources, opportunities, and wealth for everyone. It's the opposite of a scarcity mentality, which is the belief that resources are limited and that success must come at the expense of others. Cultivating an abundance mentality is crucial for achieving financial freedom because it allows you to see opportunities where others see limitations and to approach life with a sense of optimism and possibility.

One of the key ways to cultivate an abundance mentality is to practice gratitude. When you focus on what you have rather than what you lack, you begin to see the abundance in your life. Gratitude helps shift your focus from scarcity to abundance and opens your mind to new possibilities. Make it a daily practice to reflect on the things you are grateful for, whether it's your health, relationships, career, or financial situation. By focusing on the positive aspects of your life, you can cultivate a mindset of abundance.

Another way to develop an abundance mentality is to give generously. When you give your time, energy, or money to others, you reinforce the belief that there is enough to go around. Giving creates a sense of abundance because it reminds you that you have something valuable to offer and that your contributions make a difference. Whether it's volunteering your time, donating to a cause you care about, or helping a friend in need, giving is a powerful way to cultivate an abundance mentality.

It's also important to avoid comparing yourself to others. In today's social media-driven world, it's easy to fall into the trap of comparing your financial situation to that of others. However, comparison often leads to feelings of inadequacy and scarcity. Instead of comparing yourself to others, focus on your own journey and celebrate your progress. Remember that everyone's financial situation is different, and what matters most is your own growth and success.

Lastly, surround yourself with abundance-minded people. Just as with overcoming limiting beliefs, the people you spend time with can influence your mindset. Seek out individuals who have an abundance mentality, who are optimistic and generous, and who inspire you to see the possibilities in your own life. By surrounding yourself with positive influences, you can reinforce your own abundance mindset.

The Psychology of Money

The psychology of money refers to the way our thoughts, emotions, and behaviors influence our financial decisions. Understanding the psychology of money is essential for achieving financial freedom because it helps you recognize the patterns and habits that may be holding you back and allows you to make more informed and rational decisions.

One of the key concepts in the psychology of money is the idea of financial self-concept. Your financial self-concept is the way you see yourself in relation to money. It's shaped by your upbringing, experiences, and beliefs, and it influences how you manage your finances. For example, if you see yourself as someone who is "bad with money," you may be more likely to avoid financial planning, make impulsive purchases, or fail to save for the future. On the other hand, if you see yourself as someone who is financially savvy, you may be more likely to budget, invest, and make thoughtful financial decisions.

To improve your financial self-concept, start by examining the beliefs and experiences that have shaped your relationship with money. Consider how your parents or caregivers handled money, the messages you received about money growing up, and any significant financial experiences you've had. Once you have a better understanding of your financial self-concept, you can begin to challenge and change any negative beliefs or behaviors that are holding you back.

Another important aspect of the psychology of money is the role of emotions in financial decision-making. Emotions such as fear, greed, and guilt can have a powerful impact on how you manage your finances. For example, fear of losing money might prevent you from investing, while greed could lead you to take on excessive risk in pursuit of higher returns. Understanding how emotions influence your financial decisions can help you make more rational and informed choices.

One way to manage your emotions around money is to develop a financial plan. A financial plan provides a roadmap for your financial future and helps you stay focused on your long-term goals. When you have a clear plan in place, you are less likely to make impulsive or emotionally-driven decisions. Additionally, having a plan can help reduce financial stress and anxiety, as you have a clear path to follow and can measure your progress along the way.

Finally, understanding the psychology of money involves recognizing the impact of cognitive biases on your financial decisions. Cognitive biases are mental shortcuts that can lead to irrational or flawed decision-making. Some common cognitive biases that affect financial decisions include the following:

Loss Aversion: The tendency to fear losses more than valuing gains. This bias can lead to overly conservative investment decisions or an unwillingness to sell losing investments.

Overconfidence: The tendency to overestimate your knowledge or abilities. This bias can lead to taking on excessive risk or making uninformed financial decisions.

Anchoring: The tendency to rely too heavily on the first piece of information you receive when making a decision. This bias can lead to poor financial decisions if the initial information is incorrect or incomplete.

By becoming aware of these cognitive biases, you can take steps to mitigate their impact on your financial decisions. This might involve seeking out additional information, consulting with a financial advisor, or taking a step back to reflect before making important financial decisions.

Defining Your Financial Goals

Once you have laid the mental foundation for financial freedom by adopting a wealth mindset, overcoming limiting beliefs, cultivating an abundance mentality, and understanding the psychology of money, the next step is to define your financial goals. Setting clear, specific goals is essential for achieving financial freedom because it gives you a target to work towards and helps you stay focused on your financial journey. Without clear goals, it's easy to get sidetracked or lose motivation, but with well-defined objectives, you can measure your progress and make adjustments as needed.

When defining your financial goals, it's important to start by reflecting on what you truly want to achieve with your money. Financial goals should align with your personal values, lifestyle aspirations, and long-term vision for your life. Consider what financial freedom means to you: Is it the ability to retire early? Is it owning a home, starting a business, or traveling the world? Your financial goals should reflect your deepest desires and the life you want to create for yourself.

To begin, take some time to brainstorm and write down your financial goals. Don't worry about whether they seem too ambitious or too modest—this is just the initial step of getting your thoughts on paper. After you've listed your goals, the next step is to organize them into categories, such as short-term, medium-term, and long term goals. This will help you prioritize and create a roadmap for achieving each one.

Setting SMART Financial Goals

Once you've identified your financial goals, the next step is to ensure they are SMART: Specific, Measurable, Achievable, Relevant, and Time-bound. SMART goals provide a clear framework that makes it easier to track your progress and stay committed to your objectives.

Specific: Your financial goals should be clear and specific. Instead of setting a vague goal like "I want to save money," make it specific by stating, "I want to save $10,000 for a down payment on a house." Specific goals provide a clear direction and make it easier to create a plan to achieve them.

Measurable: A measurable goal is one that you can track over time. This involves setting criteria for measuring progress, such as "I will save $500 each month until I reach $10,000." Measurable goals allow you to see how far you've come and help you stay motivated as you get closer to achieving them.

Achievable: While it's important to set ambitious goals, they should also be realistic and achievable based on your current financial situation. Setting an unrealistic goal can lead to frustration and discouragement. To determine if your goal is achievable, consider your income, expenses, and other financial obligations.

Relevant: Your financial goals should align with your overall life objectives and be relevant to your personal values and priorities. For example, if one of your core values is financial security, setting a goal to build an emergency fund would be highly relevant. A relevant goal ensures that your efforts are focused on what truly matters to you.

Time-bound: A time-bound goal has a specific deadline or timeframe for completion. This creates a sense of urgency and helps you stay focused on your goal. For example, "I want to save $10,000 for a down payment on a house within the next 24 months" is a time-bound goal. Setting a deadline helps you plan your actions and stay on track to achieve your objective.

By setting SMART financial goals, you give yourself a clear roadmap for achieving financial freedom. These goals act as milestones on your journey, guiding your decisions and actions along the way. As you achieve each goal, you'll build momentum and confidence, which will propel you towards even greater financial success.

ShortTerm vs. LongTerm Goals

As you set your financial goals, it's important to distinguish between shortterm and longterm objectives. Both types of goals are crucial for building financial freedom, but they require different strategies and timelines.

ShortTerm Goals: Short-term goals are those you aim to achieve within the next year or two. These goals are often more immediate and can include things like paying off credit card debt, saving for a vacation, or building an emergency fund. Because short-term goals have a relatively quick turnaround, they typically require more focused effort and disciplined budgeting. The key to achieving short-term goals is to prioritize them in your daily financial decisions. For example, you might need to cut back on discretionary spending or take on a side hustle to reach your short-term savings targets.

LongTerm Goals: Long-term goals are those that take several years or even decades to achieve. These goals are often larger in scale and require sustained effort over a longer period of time. Examples of long-term goals include saving for retirement, paying off a mortgage, or building a significant investment portfolio. Achieving long-term goals requires patience, consistency, and a well-thought out financial plan. Because these goals span a longer timeframe, they benefit from the power of compound interest and incremental progress. For example, contributing regularly to a retirement account over many years can result in significant growth thanks to compounding returns.

Balancing shortterm and longterm goals is key to financial success. While it's important to focus on immediate financial needs, you should also keep your eye on the bigger picture. One strategy is to divide your savings and investment contributions between shortterm and longterm goals. For instance, you might allocate a portion of your monthly income to a short-term savings account for an upcoming vacation, while also contributing to a retirement account for the long term.

By setting both shortterm and longterm goals, you create a comprehensive financial plan that addresses your immediate needs while also securing your financial future. This balanced approach helps ensure that you are making progress on multiple fronts and that you are prepared for both near-term and distant financial challenges.

The Importance of Vision and Purpose

A crucial aspect of setting the foundation for financial freedom is understanding the importance of vision and purpose. Your vision is your long-term view of what you want your life to look like, and your purpose is the underlying reason behind your financial goals. Together, they provide direction and motivation for your financial journey.

Vision: Your financial vision is a clear and compelling picture of your desired future. It's about envisioning the lifestyle you want to lead, the opportunities you want to create, and the impact you want to have. A strong vision serves as a guiding star, helping you stay focused on your long-term goals even when faced with short-term challenges. To create a vision, take some time to reflect on what financial freedom means to you. Where do you see yourself in 10, 20, or 30 years? What kind of life do you want to build? Write down your vision in as much detail as possible, and revisit it regularly to keep yourself motivated and aligned with your goals.

Purpose: Your purpose is the "why" behind your financial goals. It's the deeper motivation that drives you to achieve financial freedom. Purpose is what gives your goals meaning and significance. For example, your purpose might be to provide financial security for your family, to achieve independence from a job you don't enjoy, or to make a positive impact on your community. Understanding your purpose helps you stay committed to your goals, even when the journey gets tough. It reminds you that your financial efforts are about more than just accumulating money—they are about creating a life that aligns with your values and aspirations.

Combining vision and purpose with your financial goals creates a powerful foundation for success. When your goals are connected to a clear vision and a strong purpose, they become more than just targets to hit they become steps on the path to your ideal life. This connection between vision, purpose, and goals ensures that your financial journey is not just about numbers, but about living a life that is true to who you are and what you want to achieve.

In conclusion, setting the foundation for financial freedom involves more than just managing money; it's about cultivating the right mindset, overcoming limiting beliefs, understanding the psychology of money, and defining clear, meaningful goals. By setting SMART financial goals, balancing shortterm and longterm objectives, and grounding your financial journey in a strong vision and purpose, you can create a roadmap to financial freedom that is both achievable and deeply fulfilling. This foundation will support you as you work toward the financial independence you desire, guiding you through challenges and helping you stay focused on your ultimate destination.

Chapter 2

Building a Strong Financial Base

Achieving financial freedom requires a strong financial base, much like building a house requires a solid foundation. Without a firm financial base, even the best-laid financial plans can crumble under the pressure of unexpected expenses, debt, or poor money management. In this chapter, we will explore the essential components of building a strong financial foundation, including budgeting basics, creating a sustainable budget, tracking your income and expenses, and understanding the importance of an emergency fund. We will also discuss debt management, including the difference between good debt and bad debt, strategies for paying off debt, and how to avoid common debt traps.

Budgeting Basics

Budgeting is the cornerstone of financial management. A budget is a plan for how you will allocate your income to cover your expenses, save for the future, and achieve your financial goals. Without a budget, it's easy to lose track of where your money is going and to spend beyond your means. A well-crafted budget helps you take control of your finances, ensuring that you are living within your means and making progress toward your financial goals.

The first step in creating a budget is to understand your income. This includes your regular paycheck as well as any additional sources of income, such as side jobs, investments, or rental income. Once you have a clear picture of your total income, the next step is to categorize your expenses. Expenses can be divided into fixed and variable categories:

Fixed Expenses: These are the expenses that remain relatively constant each month, such as rent or mortgage payments, utilities, insurance premiums, and loan payments.

Variable Expenses: These are expenses that can fluctuate from month to month, such as groceries, entertainment, dining out, and transportation costs.

After categorizing your expenses, it's important to subtract your total expenses from your total income to determine whether you have a surplus or a deficit. If you have a surplus, you can allocate this extra money toward savings, investments, or debt repayment. If you have a deficit, it's time to look for areas where you can cut back on spending.

Creating a Sustainable Budget

A sustainable budget is one that you can realistically stick to over the long term. It's not about depriving yourself of all enjoyment or living a life of extreme frugality; rather, it's about finding a balance that allows you to meet your financial obligations, save for the future, and still enjoy your life.

To create a sustainable budget, start by setting realistic spending limits for each category of expenses. For example, if you've been spending $300 a month on dining out, but you know you need to cut back, set a budget of $200 and find ways to enjoy meals at home or seek out more affordable dining options. It's important to set limits that challenge you to be mindful of your spending but are also achievable, so you don't feel discouraged.

Another key aspect of a sustainable budget is flexibility. Life is unpredictable, and there will be months when unexpected expenses arise. A good budget allows for some flexibility, so you can adjust your spending in one area to accommodate an unexpected expense in another. For example, if your car needs repairs, you might reduce your entertainment spending that month to cover the cost.

Automating your savings and bill payments is another strategy to make your budget more sustainable. By setting up automatic transfers to your savings account and scheduling automatic bill payments, you reduce the likelihood of overspending or missing a payment. Automation helps you stay on track with your budget without having to constantly think about it.

Finally, review and adjust your budget regularly. As your income and expenses change, it's important to revisit your budget to ensure it still aligns with your financial goals. Regularly reviewing your budget also allows you to identify areas where you may be overspending and make necessary adjustments.

Tracking Your Income and Expenses

Tracking your income and expenses is an essential part of effective budgeting.

It's not enough to simply create a budget; you need to actively monitor your spending to ensure you are staying within your limits and making progress toward your goals. Tracking your finances allows you to see exactly where your money is going, identify any areas of overspending, and make informed decisions about where to cut back or reallocate funds.

There are several methods for tracking your income and expenses:

Pen and Paper: The simplest method is to record your income and expenses in a notebook or on a spreadsheet. This method requires discipline and consistency but can be effective if you prefer a hand-son approach.

Budgeting Apps: There are many budgeting apps available that can help you track your spending automatically. These apps often link to your bank accounts and credit cards, categorizing your transactions and providing you with a real-time view of your spending. Popular budgeting apps include Mint, YNAB (You Need a Budget), and PocketGuard.

Bank and Credit Card Statements: Reviewing your monthly bank and credit card statements is another way to track your spending. By regularly reviewing these statements, you can identify patterns in your spending and ensure that you are staying within your budget.

Whichever method you choose, the key is to be consistent. Tracking your income and expenses regularly—ideally on a daily or weekly basis—will give you the information you need to make informed financial decisions and adjust your budget as needed.

The 50/30/20 Rule

The 50/30/20 rule is a popular budgeting guideline that can help you allocate your income in a balanced and sustainable way. The rule suggests dividing your after-tax income into three categories:

50% for Needs: This category includes essential expenses such as housing, utilities, groceries, transportation, insurance, and minimum debt payments. These are the expenses you must cover to maintain your basic standard of living.

30% for Wants: This category includes discretionary spending on things like dining out, entertainment, vacations, and hobbies. While these expenses are not essential, they are important for your quality of life and personal enjoyment.

20% for Savings and Debt Repayment: This category includes contributions to your savings accounts, retirement funds, investments, and any extra payments toward debt. This is the portion of your income that helps you build wealth and achieve financial freedom.

The 50/30/20 rule provides a simple framework that can help you maintain a balanced budget while still allowing for flexibility. If your essential expenses exceed 50% of your income, you may need to make adjustments in other areas, such as reducing discretionary spending or finding ways to increase your income. Conversely, if your essential expenses are lower than 50%, you may have more room to allocate funds toward savings or wants.

While the 50/30/20 rule is a useful guideline, it's important to tailor it to your specific financial situation and goals. For example, if you are aggressively paying off debt or saving for a major goal, you may choose to allocate more than 20% of your income to savings and debt repayment. The key is to find a balance that works for you and supports your long-term financial objectives.

Emergency Fund Essentials

An emergency fund is a critical component of a strong financial base. It's a savings account specifically designated for unexpected expenses, such as medical emergencies, car repairs, or job loss. Having an emergency fund provides a financial safety net, allowing you to cover these unforeseen expenses without resorting to high-interest credit cards or loans.

The Importance of an Emergency Fund

An emergency fund is important because it protects you from financial setbacks that could derail your progress toward financial freedom. Without an emergency fund, even a minor unexpected expense can lead to financial stress, debt, or the need to dip into long-term savings. By having an emergency fund in place, you can handle these situations with confidence, knowing that you have the resources to cover unexpected costs without jeopardizing your financial goals.

An emergency fund also provides peace of mind. Knowing that you have a financial cushion can reduce stress and anxiety about the "what-ifs" in life. It allows you to focus on your financial goals without constantly worrying about potential setbacks.

How Much Should You Save?

The amount you should save in your emergency fund depends on your individual circumstances, including your income, expenses, and risk factors.

A common recommendation is to save three to six months' worth of living expenses. This means that if your monthly expenses total $3,000, you should aim to save between $9,000 and $18,000 in your emergency fund.

If you have a stable job, dual-income household, or low monthly expenses, you may be comfortable with a smaller emergency fund, closer to three months' worth of expenses. On the other hand, if you have an unstable income, are self-employed, or have high monthly expenses, you may want to aim for a larger emergency fund, closer to six months' worth of expenses or more.

Ultimately, the right amount for your emergency fund is the amount that allows you to feel secure and confident in your ability to handle unexpected expenses. It's better to start with a smaller goal and build up your emergency fund over time than to feel overwhelmed by the prospect of saving a large sum all at once.

Strategies for Building Your Fund Quickly

Building an emergency fund takes time, but there are several strategies you can use to accelerate the process:

Automate Your Savings: Set up automatic transfers from your checking account to your emergency fund savings account. This ensures that you consistently save money each month without having to think about it. Even small, regular contributions can add up over time.

Cut Unnecessary Expenses: Review your budget for areas where you can cut back on discretionary spending. Redirect the money you save toward your emergency fund. For example, you might reduce dining out, cancel unused subscriptions, or limit entertainment expenses.

Use Windfalls Wisely: If you receive unexpected money, such as a tax refund, bonus, or gift, consider putting it directly into your emergency fund. Windfalls provide an excellent opportunity to make significant progress toward your savings goal.

Take on a Side Hustle: Earning extra income through a side job or freelance work can significantly boost your emergency fund. Even part-time work or monetizing a hobby can provide additional cash that you can funnel directly into your savings.

Sell Unused Items: Declutter your home and sell items you no longer need or use. Online platforms like eBay, Facebook Marketplace, or local garage sales can help you turn unused goods into cash that you can deposit into your emergency fund.

Adjust Your Withholding: If you typically receive a large tax refund, consider adjusting your tax withholding so that you have more money in each paycheck. Instead of waiting for a lump sum at tax time, you can save this extra income throughout the year, boosting your emergency fund more quickly.

Set MicroGoals: Breaking down your savings goal into smaller, manageable milestones can make the process less daunting. For example, if your goal is to save $10,000, start by aiming to save the first $1,000, then the next $1,000, and so on. Celebrate each milestone to stay motivated.

By implementing these strategies, you can build your emergency fund more quickly and strengthen your financial foundation. Remember, the key to building an emergency fund is consistency. Even if you start small, regular contributions over time will help you achieve your savings goal.

Debt Management

Debt management is another critical aspect of building a strong financial base. While debt can be a useful financial tool when used wisely, it can also be a significant burden if not managed properly. Understanding the difference between good debt and bad debt, as well as developing strategies for paying off debt, is essential for achieving financial freedom.

Understanding Good Debt vs. Bad Debt

Not all debt is created equal. Some types of debt can help you build wealth and achieve your financial goals, while others can hinder your progress and create financial stress. Understanding the difference between good debt and bad debt is crucial for effective debt management.

Good Debt: Good debt is typically used to finance investments that have the potential to increase in value or generate income over time. Examples of good debt include student loans (if they lead to a higher-paying job), mortgages (as they allow you to build equity in a home), and business loans (if they fund a profitable venture). Good debt should have manageable interest rates and should be taken on with a clear plan for repayment.

Bad Debt: Bad debt, on the other hand, is typically used to finance consumption rather than investment. It includes high-interest debt, such as credit card balances, payday loans, and auto loans for luxury vehicles. Bad debt can quickly spiral out of control, leading to financial stress and difficulty achieving your financial goals. It often comes with high interest rates that make it difficult to pay off the principal balance.

The key to managing debt is to focus on minimizing or eliminating bad debt while strategically using good debt to build wealth. This involves being mindful of how you use credit and making informed decisions about borrowing.

Strategies for Paying Off Debt

If you currently have debt, developing a plan to pay it off is essential for achieving financial freedom. There are several strategies you can use to eliminate debt, depending on your financial situation and personal preferences:

The Debt Snowball Method: The debt snowball method involves paying off your debts from smallest to largest balance, regardless of interest rate. Start by making minimum payments on all your debts except the smallest one, which you pay off as quickly as possible. Once the smallest debt is paid off, move on to the next smallest debt, and so on. This method can provide quick wins and build momentum, keeping you motivated as you see your debts disappear one by one.

The Debt Avalanche Method: The debt avalanche method focuses on paying off debts with the highest interest rates first. This approach saves you the most money in interest over time. Like the snowball method, you make minimum payments on all your debts except the one with the highest interest rate, which you pay off aggressively.

Once the highest-interest debt is eliminated, move on to the next highest interest rate, and continue the process until all debts are paid off.

Debt Consolidation: Debt consolidation involves combining multiple debts into a single loan or payment with a lower interest rate. This can simplify your payments and potentially reduce your overall interest costs. Common methods of debt consolidation include personal loans, balance transfer credit cards, and home equity loans. However, it's important to be cautious with debt consolidation, as it doesn't eliminate the underlying debt, and you need to avoid accumulating new debt after consolidation.

Negotiate with Creditors: If you're struggling to keep up with debt payments, consider negotiating with your creditors. In some cases, they may be willing to lower your interest rate, reduce your monthly payment, or settle your debt for a lump sum that's less than the total amount owed. While negotiating can be challenging, it can provide relief and make your debt more manageable.

Increase Your Income: One of the most effective ways to pay off debt faster is to increase your income. This could involve taking on a second job, freelancing, or starting a side business. The additional income can be used to make extra payments toward your debt, helping you pay it off more quickly and reduce the amount of interest you pay.

Cut Expenses: Reducing your expenses can free up more money to put toward your debt. Review your budget and look for areas where you can cut back, such as dining out, subscriptions, or discretionary spending. Redirect these savings toward your debt payments to accelerate your progress.

Avoiding Debt Traps

While managing existing debt is important, it's equally crucial to avoid falling into new debt traps. Debt traps can occur when you take on new debt without a clear plan for repayment or when you rely on credit to cover basic living expenses. Here are some strategies for avoiding common debt traps:

Live Within Your Means: The most effective way to avoid debt traps is to live within your means. This means ensuring that your spending aligns with your income and that you're not relying on credit to cover everyday expenses. If you find yourself consistently using credit to make ends meet, it may be time to reevaluate your budget and look for ways to cut back on spending or increase your income.

Avoid HighInterest Debt: High-interest debt, such as credit card balances or payday loans, can quickly become unmanageable. To avoid falling into a debt trap, avoid carrying a balance on high-interest credit cards, and steer clear of predatory lenders that charge exorbitant interest rates. If you do need to use credit, aim to pay off the balance in full each month to avoid interest charges.

Build an Emergency Fund: An emergency fund is your first line of defense against falling into debt. By having a financial cushion to cover unexpected expenses, you can avoid resorting to credit cards or loans in a crisis. Make building and maintaining an emergency fund a priority to protect yourself from future debt.

Be Cautious with Borrowing: Before taking on new debt, carefully consider whether it's truly necessary and how it will impact your financial situation. Avoid borrowing for nonessential purchases, and only take on debt that you can comfortably afford to repay. Make sure you understand the terms of any loan or credit agreement, including the interest rate, fees, and repayment schedule.

Use Credit Wisely: If you use credit cards, do so responsibly. Pay off the balance in full each month to avoid interest charges, and only use credit for purchases you can afford to pay off immediately. Avoid maxing out your credit cards, as high credit utilization can negatively impact your credit score.

Stay Educated About Personal Finance: Continuing to educate yourself about personal finance can help you make informed decisions and avoid common pitfalls. Understanding how interest rates, credit scores, and loan terms work can empower you to make smart borrowing decisions and avoid debt traps.

In conclusion, building a strong financial base is essential for achieving financial freedom. By mastering the basics of budgeting, tracking your income and expenses, and following guidelines like the 50/30/20 rule, you can create a sustainable financial plan that supports your goals. Establishing an emergency fund provides a safety net for unexpected expenses, while effective debt management strategies help you eliminate existing debt and avoid falling into new debt traps. With a strong financial foundation in place, you can confidently move forward on your journey to financial independence, knowing that you have the tools and knowledge to navigate any challenges that come your way.

Chapter 3

Maximizing Income

Building a strong financial base is only one part of achieving financial freedom. To truly transform your financial situation, you need to focus on maximizing your income. While cutting expenses and managing debt are important, increasing your income can provide you with the resources to save, invest, and reach your financial goals faster. In this chapter, we'll explore various strategies to maximize your income, including career growth, developing marketable skills, negotiating your salary, leveraging side hustles and multiple income streams, and pursuing entrepreneurship and passive income opportunities.

Career Growth Strategies

Your career is likely one of your primary sources of income, making it a key area to focus on when looking to maximize your earnings. A well-planned career strategy can lead to promotions, raises, and opportunities that significantly increase your income over time. Here are some strategies to help you grow your career and maximize your earning potential:

Set Clear Career Goals: Start by defining your long-term career goals. What position or level do you want to achieve? What type of work are you passionate about? By setting clear goals, you can create a roadmap for your career and identify the steps needed to reach your objectives.

Seek Out Growth Opportunities: Look for opportunities within your current organization to grow and take on more responsibility. This could involve volunteering for challenging projects, leading a team, or taking on a role that stretches your skills. By demonstrating your value and willingness to grow, you increase your chances of being considered for promotions or raises.

Continuously Improve Your Skills: The job market is constantly evolving, and staying competitive requires a commitment to continuous learning. Identify the skills that are in demand in your industry and invest in developing them. This could involve taking courses, attending workshops, earning certifications, or pursuing higher education. By continuously improving your skills, you make yourself more valuable to your employer and increase your chances of commanding a higher salary.

Network and Build Relationships: Networking is a powerful tool for career growth. Building strong relationships with colleagues, industry peers, and mentors can open doors to new opportunities. Attend industry conferences, join professional organizations, and actively engage with others in your field. A strong professional network can provide you with valuable insights, job referrals, and opportunities for advancement.

Seek Feedback and Act on It: Regularly seek feedback from your supervisors, peers, and mentors to identify areas where you can improve. Constructive feedback can help you refine your skills and address any weaknesses that may be holding you back. Actively working on the areas highlighted in feedback demonstrates your commitment to growth and can lead to career advancement.

Be Proactive About Advancement: Don't wait for opportunities to come to you—be proactive in seeking out new roles, responsibilities, and challenges. If you believe you're ready for a promotion or raise, prepare a strong case that highlights your achievements and the value you bring to the organization. Present this case to your supervisor and express your interest in advancing your career.

Building Marketable Skills

In today's competitive job market, having a set of marketable skills can significantly enhance your earning potential. Marketable skills are those that are in high demand by employers and can differentiate you from other candidates. Here are some strategies for building and enhancing your marketable skills:

Identify InDemand Skills: Research your industry to identify the skills that are most sought after by employers. These could include technical skills, such as programming or data analysis, as well as soft skills, such as communication, leadership, and problem-solving. Focus on developing the skills that are most relevant to your career goals.

Invest in Education and Training: Continuous education is key to building marketable skills. Consider enrolling in courses, workshops, or certification programs that align with your career goals. Online learning platforms like Coursera, Udemy, and LinkedIn Learning offer a wide range of courses that can help you develop new skills at your own pace.

Gain Practical Experience: Practical experience is often the best way to develop and refine your skills. Look for opportunities to apply your skills in real-world settings, whether through your current job, internships, volunteer work, or freelance projects. Handson experience not only enhances your skills but also provides you with tangible examples of your work that you can showcase to potential employers.

Stay Current with Industry Trends: The skills that are in demand today may not be the same in the future. Stay informed about the latest trends and developments in your industry to ensure that your skills remain relevant. Subscribe to industry publications, follow thought leaders on social media, and participate in professional development opportunities to stay ahead of the curve.

Develop a Portfolio: If your field involves creative or technical work, building a portfolio can be a powerful way to showcase your skills. A well-curated portfolio demonstrates your capabilities to potential employers or clients and provides concrete evidence of your expertise. Include examples of your best work, along with descriptions of the skills you used to complete each project.

Cultivate Soft Skills: While technical skills are important, don't overlook the value of soft skills. Employers highly value employees who can communicate effectively, work well in teams, and demonstrate leadership. These skills can often be the deciding factor in whether you're chosen for a promotion or new job opportunity.

Negotiating Your Salary

Negotiating your salary is one of the most effective ways to increase your income. Many employees miss out on higher earnings simply because they don't negotiate or don't know how to negotiate effectively. Here are some tips to help you negotiate your salary with confidence:

Research Your Market Value: Before entering a salary negotiation, research the average salary for your position and level of experience in your industry and location. Websites like Glassdoor, Payscale, and LinkedIn Salary can provide valuable data to help you determine a fair salary range. Knowing your market value gives you a strong foundation for negotiation.

Highlight Your Achievements: When negotiating your salary, it's important to demonstrate the value you bring to the organization. Prepare a list of your key achievements, contributions, and any metrics that showcase your impact. Be ready to discuss how your skills and experience have benefited the company and how you will continue to add value in the future.

Practice Your Negotiation Skills: Negotiation can be intimidating, especially if you're not used to advocating for yourself. Practice your negotiation skills with a friend, mentor, or coach to build your confidence. Roleplaying different scenarios can help you prepare for potential objections and refine your approach.

Be Willing to Walk Away: While it's important to negotiate assertively, it's also important to know your limits. If the offer doesn't meet your expectations and you have other opportunities or feel confident in your ability to find a better offer, be prepared to walk away. Sometimes, the willingness to walk away can lead to a better offer, as it shows you know your worth.

Consider the Whole Compensation Package: Salary is just one component of your compensation package. When negotiating, consider other benefits such as bonuses, stock options, retirement contributions, health insurance, and paid time off. If the employer is unable to meet your salary expectations, you may be able to negotiate for additional benefits that enhance your overall compensation.

Stay Professional and Positive: Approach salary negotiations with a positive and collaborative mindset. Express your appreciation for the offer and frame the negotiation as a discussion about mutual benefit—how you can continue to contribute to the company's success and how the company can fairly compensate you for your contributions. A professional and positive approach can lead to a more successful negotiation outcome.

Side Hustles and Multiple Income Streams

Relying solely on one source of income can be risky, especially in today's uncertain economic environment. Diversifying your income by developing side hustles and multiple income streams can provide financial security and help you achieve your financial goals faster. Here's how to get started:

Identify Your Skills and Interests: The first step in developing a side hustle is to identify your skills, interests, and passions. What do you enjoy doing in your spare time? What skills do you have that others might be willing to pay for? Your side hustle should ideally align with your interests and strengths, as this will increase your chances of success and make the work more enjoyable.

Research Market Demand: Once you've identified potential side hustle ideas, research the market demand for those services or products. Are there others offering similar services? What are customers willing to pay? Understanding the market demand will help you refine your side hustle idea and identify opportunities for differentiation.

Start Small and Test the Waters: You don't need to quit your day job to start a side hustle. Start small by offering your services or products on a part-time basis, and test the waters to see if there's demand. This approach allows you to build your side hustle gradually without taking on too much risk.

Leverage Online Platforms: The internet has made it easier than ever to start a side hustle. Online platforms like Etsy, Fiverr, Upwork, and Amazon allow you to reach a global audience and sell your products or services with minimal upfront investment. Leverage these platforms to market your side hustle and reach potential customers.

Manage Your Time Effectively: Balancing a side hustle with your full-time job requires effective time management. Set clear boundaries and create a schedule that allows you to work on your side hustle without neglecting your primary job or personal life. Use tools like calendars, task lists, and time-tracking apps to stay organized and productive.

Scale Your Side Hustle: If your side hustle becomes successful, consider ways to scale it into a more significant income stream. This could involve outsourcing certain tasks, investing in marketing, or expanding your product or service offerings. Scaling your side hustle can turn it into a substantial source of income and even lead to full-time entrepreneurship.

Entrepreneurship and Passive Income

Entrepreneurship and passive income are powerful avenues for maximizing your income and achieving financial freedom. While entrepreneurship involves actively building and managing a business, passive income allows you to earn money with minimal ongoing effort. In this section, we'll explore how to start your own business, invest in real estate, and generate multiple streams of passive income.

Starting Your Own Business

Starting a business can be a rewarding way to take control of your financial future and create wealth. However, it requires careful planning, dedication, and a willingness to take risks. Here are some key steps to consider when starting your own business:

Identify a Profitable Business Idea: The foundation of any successful business is a strong idea that meets a market need. Consider your skills, experience, and passions, and think about how they can be turned into a profitable business. Research the market to identify gaps or unmet needs that your business could address. Look for trends and emerging industries that offer growth potential.

Create a Business Plan: A solid business plan is essential for guiding your business's growth and securing funding. Your business plan should include an overview of your business concept, a market analysis, a description of your products or services, a marketing strategy, an operational plan, and financial projections. A well-thoughtout business plan helps you clarify your goals and provides a roadmap for success.

Secure Funding: Depending on the nature of your business, you may need to secure funding to cover startup costs. This could involve using your savings, securing a loan, or seeking investors. Explore different funding options, such as small business loans, grants, crowdfunding, or angel investors. Make sure you have a clear understanding of your financial needs and create a budget to manage your expenses.

Choose the Right Business Structure: The legal structure of your business affects everything from taxes to liability. Common business structures include sole proprietorships, partnerships, limited liability companies (LLCs), and corporations. Each structure has its advantages and disadvantages, so it's important to choose the one that best suits your needs and longterm goals. Consider consulting with a lawyer or accountant to determine the best structure for your business.

Build Your Brand: Your brand is how your business is perceived by customers and the public. It includes your business name, logo, website, and overall image. Invest time and resources into creating a strong brand that resonates with your target audience. Your brand should reflect your business values, mission, and unique selling points.

Market Your Business: Marketing is essential for attracting customers and generating sales. Develop a marketing strategy that includes both online and offline tactics. Utilize social media, search engine optimization (SEO), content marketing, and paid advertising to reach your target audience. Don't underestimate the power of word of mouth marketing and networking to build your customer base.

Manage and Scale Your Business: Once your business is up and running, focus on managing your operations efficiently and scaling your growth. This may involve hiring employees, expanding your product or service offerings, entering new markets, or investing in technology. Monitor your financial performance and make data-driven decisions to ensure your business remains profitable and sustainable.

Investing in Real Estate

Real estate has long been considered one of the most reliable ways to build wealth and generate passive income. Whether you're interested in residential or commercial properties, real estate offers numerous opportunities to maximize your income. Here's how to get started with real estate investing:

Understand the Basics of Real Estate Investing: Before diving into real estate, it's important to educate yourself about the different types of real estate investments, such as rental properties, fix and flip projects, and real estate investment trusts (REITs). Each type of investment has its own risks, rewards, and management requirements. Understanding the basics will help you choose the best investment strategy for your goals.

Choose the Right Property: Location is one of the most critical factors in real estate investing. Look for properties in areas with strong demand, potential for appreciation, and access to amenities like schools, transportation, and shopping. Conduct a thorough analysis of the property, including its condition, potential rental income, and costs for repairs or renovations. Working with a real estate agent or property manager can help you find the right property and negotiate a fair price.

Secure Financing: Real estate investing typically requires a significant upfront investment, so securing financing is an important step. Explore different financing options, such as traditional mortgages, hard money loans, or private investors. Make sure you understand the terms and interest rates of your loan, and calculate your potential return on investment (ROI) to ensure the property is a sound investment.

Generate Rental Income: One of the most common ways to generate passive income through real estate is by renting out your property. Rental income can provide a steady cash flow and help you pay off your mortgage while building equity. To maximize your rental income, set competitive rental rates, screen tenants carefully, and maintain the property to keep it in good condition. Consider hiring a property management company to handle daytoday operations, especially if you own multiple properties or live far from the rental property.

Consider House Hacking: House hacking is a strategy where you buy a property, live in one part of it, and rent out the other parts to generate income. This could involve renting out rooms in a single-family home or purchasing a multiunit property and living in one of the units. House hacking can significantly reduce your housing costs and provide a pathway to building wealth through real estate.

Invest in Real Estate Crowd-funding: If you're interested in real estate but don't want to manage properties directly, real estate crowdfunding offers an alternative. Through crowdfunding platforms, you can invest in real estate projects with a lower initial investment and earn a share of the profits. This approach allows you to diversify your real estate portfolio and access opportunities that may not be available through traditional real estate investing.

Understand the Risks: Real estate investing, like any investment, carries risks. Market fluctuations, property damage, and tenant issues can impact your income and profitability. It's important to have a clear understanding of the risks involved and to have a contingency plan in place. Diversifying your investments and maintaining a healthy cash reserve can help you manage these risks effectively.

Generating Passive Income Streams

Passive income is money earned with little to no ongoing effort. It's a powerful way to build wealth and achieve financial freedom, as it allows you to earn money while focusing on other activities. Here are some strategies for generating passive income:

Dividend Stocks: Investing in dividend-paying stocks allows you to earn regular income without selling your shares. Companies that pay dividends distribute a portion of their profits to shareholders, providing you with a steady income stream. Look for high-quality, dividend-paying companies with a history of stable or growing dividends. Reinvesting your dividends can further accelerate your wealth-building efforts.

Real Estate Investment Trusts (REITs): REITs are companies that own and operate income-producing real estate, such as commercial properties, apartment buildings, and shopping centers. By investing in REITs, you can earn passive income through dividends paid by the trust. REITs offer a way to invest in real estate without the need to manage properties directly, making them an attractive option for passive income.

Peer to Peer Lending: Peer To Peer (P2P) lending platforms allow you to lend money to individuals or businesses in exchange for interest payments. By investing in P2P loans, you can earn passive income from the interest paid by borrowers. However, it's important to be aware of the risks, as some borrowers may default on their loans. Diversifying your investments across multiple loans can help mitigate this risk.

Create and Sell Digital Products: If you have expertise in a particular area, consider creating digital products, such as ebooks, online courses, or software, that can be sold online. Once created, digital products can generate passive income with minimal ongoing effort.

Platforms like Amazon Kindle Direct Publishing, Udemy, and Shopify make it easy to market and sell digital products to a global audience.

Affiliate Marketing: Affiliate marketing involves promoting products or services on your website, blog, or social media channels and earning a commission for each sale made through your referral link. By partnering with companies that offer affiliate programs, you can earn passive income by recommending products or services that align with your audience's interests. Building a strong online presence and creating high-quality content are key to success in affiliate marketing.

Invest in Bonds: Bonds are debt securities issued by governments or corporations that pay interest over time. By investing in bonds, you can earn a fixed income stream through regular interest payments. Bonds are generally considered lower-risk investments compared to stocks, making them a suitable option for conservative investors seeking passive income.

Create an Online Business: Starting an online business, such as an ecommerce store, dropshipping business, or subscription service, can generate passive income once it's established. While building an online business requires initial effort and investment, it can provide a scalable income stream with minimal ongoing management. Automating key processes, such as order fulfillment and customer service, can further enhance the passive nature of the income.

Royalties from Intellectual Property: If you create intellectual property, such as books, music, patents, or trademarks, you can earn royalties whenever your work is used or sold. Licensing your intellectual property to others can provide a steady stream of passive income. For example, authors can earn royalties from book sales, musicians can earn royalties from song plays, and inventors can earn royalties from patented products.

The Power of Multiple Income Streams

One of the most important takeaways from this chapter is the value of diversifying your income streams. Relying on a single source of income can be risky, especially in times of economic uncertainty or job instability.

By cultivating multiple streams of income, you can reduce your financial vulnerability and create a more robust financial foundation.

Multiple income streams can come from various sources, including your primary job, side hustles, investments, and passive income opportunities. Each additional income stream contributes to your overall financial stability and can help you achieve your financial goals faster. For example, you might work a fulltime job while running a small business on the side, investing in dividend paying stocks, and earning rental income from a property. Together, these income streams provide a safety net and allow you to take calculated risks with your money.

Investing in Yourself

Maximizing your income often starts with investing in yourself. This means continuously developing your skills, expanding your knowledge, and staying adaptable in a rapidly changing world. Whether through formal education, online courses, networking, or self study, investing in your personal and professional growth is one of the best ways to increase your earning potential over the long term.

Investing in yourself also involves taking care of your health, both physically and mentally. A healthy lifestyle enables you to perform at your best, whether in your career, business, or other income generating activities. Prioritizing self-care and maintaining a work-life balance will help you sustain the energy and focus needed to pursue your financial goals effectively.

Strategic Planning and Goal Setting

To maximize your income effectively, it's crucial to have a clear plan and set specific, measurable, achievable, relevant, and timebound (SMART) financial goals. Whether your goal is to increase your salary by a certain percentage, launch a successful side business, or generate a specific amount of passive income, having a well-defined plan will guide your efforts and keep you on track.

Strategic planning involves setting shortterm and longterm goals, identifying the steps needed to achieve them, and regularly reviewing your progress. By breaking down your larger financial goals into smaller, actionable steps, you can make steady progress and celebrate your achievements along the way. This approach helps you stay motivated and focused, even when faced with challenges or setbacks.

Embracing Change and Innovation

In today's fast-paced world, change is inevitable. Those who embrace change and innovation are often better positioned to maximize their income and achieve financial success. Whether it's adopting new technologies, exploring emerging industries, or pivoting your career in response to market trends, staying open to change can create new opportunities for growth and income generation.

Innovation also involves thinking creatively about how to leverage your existing skills and resources in new ways. For example, you might explore how to turn a hobby into a profitable business, use your professional expertise to offer consulting services, or develop an online course to share your knowledge with others. By being open to new ideas and willing to take calculated risks, you can unlock new income streams and accelerate your journey toward financial freedom.

Overcoming Challenges

Maximizing your income and building wealth is not without its challenges. You may encounter obstacles such as job insecurity, market fluctuations, or personal setbacks that temporarily slow your progress. However, resilience and perseverance are key to overcoming these challenges.

It's important to approach challenges with a positive mindset and view them as opportunities for growth and learning. When faced with setbacks, take the time to reassess your goals, adjust your strategies, and seek support from mentors, peers, or professional networks. Remember that financial success is a journey, and setbacks are a natural part of that journey. By staying focused and committed, you can navigate challenges and continue making progress toward your financial goals.

Final Thoughts

Maximizing your income is a powerful tool for achieving financial freedom and creating a life of abundance. Whether through career advancement, entrepreneurship, real estate investing, or passive income generation, the strategies outlined in this chapter provide a roadmap for increasing your earning potential and building longterm wealth.

As you embark on your journey to financial freedom, remember that the key to success lies in continuous learning, strategic planning, and taking consistent action. By diversifying your income streams, investing in yourself, and embracing change, you can create a solid financial foundation that supports your dreams and aspirations.

Ultimately, the pursuit of financial freedom is about more than just money—it's about gaining the freedom to live life on your terms, pursue your passions, and make a positive impact on the world. By maximizing your income and building wealth, you can achieve the financial independence that empowers you to live a fulfilling and purposeful life.

Chapter 4

Mastering the Art of Saving

Achieving financial freedom involves more than just earning money—it also requires mastering the art of saving. Saving money is the foundation of financial security and wealth-building, enabling you to reach your financial goals, prepare for emergencies, and invest for the future. In this chapter, we'll explore advanced saving techniques, the power of compound interest, and how to make saving a seamless part of your life.

Advanced Saving Techniques

While traditional advice often focuses on basic saving strategies like cutting expenses or setting aside a percentage of your income, advanced saving techniques take a more strategic approach to accumulating wealth. These methods allow you to optimize your savings and ensure that your money is working as efficiently as possible.

Automating Your Savings: One of the most effective ways to save consistently is to automate the process. By setting up automatic transfers from your checking account to your savings account, you remove the temptation to spend that money and make saving a nonnegotiable part of your financial routine. Automation ensures that you pay yourself first, even before you have a chance to spend on discretionary items. This method is especially powerful when combined with a highinterest savings account, where your money can grow over time.

The 24-Hour Rule: The 24-hour rule is a simple yet effective strategy for avoiding impulsive spending. Before making any nonessential purchase, wait 24 hours to see if you still feel the same urge to buy. Often, you'll find that the desire to spend fades, and you can save the money instead. This technique helps you make more thoughtful decisions about your spending and prioritize saving.

Utilizing Cashback and Rewards Programs: Many credit cards and shopping apps offer cashback and rewards programs that can help you save money on everyday purchases. By using these programs strategically, you can earn money back on the items you need to buy anyway. However, it's important to use credit cards responsibly and pay off your balance in full each month to avoid interest charges that could negate your savings.

Implementing the "Pay Yourself Last" Strategy: While paying yourself first is a popular savings strategy, paying yourself last can also be effective in certain situations. This approach involves allocating money toward your financial goals after you've covered all necessary expenses and discretionary spending. The key is to find a balance that works for you—ensuring that you still prioritize saving without feeling deprived.

Sinking Funds: A sinking fund is a savings account designated for a specific future expense, such as a vacation, home renovation, or new car. By setting up sinking funds for various goals, you can save in a more organized and purposeful way. Instead of being caught off guard by large expenses, you can plan for them in advance, reducing the financial strain and avoiding debt.

Cutting Costs without Sacrificing Quality of Life

Saving money doesn't have to mean living a life of deprivation. With thoughtful planning and creativity, you can reduce your expenses without compromising your quality of life. Here are some strategies to help you cut costs while still enjoying the things that matter most:

Mindful Spending: Mindful spending involves being conscious of your spending habits and making intentional choices about where your money goes. By focusing on what truly brings you joy and value, you can eliminate unnecessary expenses and redirect those funds toward your savings. For example, instead of dining out frequently, you might choose to cook more meals at home, which can be just as enjoyable and much more cost-effective.

Negotiating Bills and Services: Many people overlook the potential savings that can come from negotiating bills and services. Whether it's your cable bill, insurance premiums, or even your rent, don't be afraid to ask for a better deal. Many companies are willing to offer discounts or match competitors' prices to retain customers. Taking the time to negotiate can result in significant savings over time.

Cutting Subscriptions and Memberships: Subscriptions and memberships can quickly add up, especially if you're not fully utilizing them. Review all your recurring expenses and cancel any subscriptions or memberships that you no longer need or use. Streaming services, gym memberships, and magazine subscriptions are common areas where people can cut costs without sacrificing much.

Energy Efficiency: Reducing your energy consumption is not only good for the environment but also for your wallet.

Simple changes like using energy-efficient light bulbs, unplugging electronics when not in use, and adjusting your thermostat can lead to substantial savings on your utility bills. Investing in energy efficient appliances can also result in long term savings.

Shopping Smart: Being a savvy shopper means looking for ways to get the best value for your money. This could involve using coupons, shopping during sales, buying in bulk, or choosing generic brands over name brands. Additionally, shopping at thrift stores or buying secondhand items can help build a solid financial foundation that supports both your short term needs and long term aspirations. Whether you're just starting out on your financial journey or looking to optimize your existing strategies, the principles covered in this chapter will help you save more effectively and achieve your financial goals faster.

The Importance of Consistency and Discipline

Saving money requires consistency and discipline. It's easy to set goals and create a savings plan, but the real challenge lies in sticking to that plan over time. Life can be unpredictable, and unexpected expenses or temptations can derail even the most well intentioned savings strategies. However, by developing strong financial habits and maintaining a disciplined approach to saving, you can overcome these challenges and stay on track.

Regular Reviews and Adjustments: Just as you would regularly review your investment portfolio, it's important to periodically assess your savings plan to ensure it's still aligned with your goals. Life changes—such as a new job, a pay raise, or a shift in your financial priorities—may require adjustments to your saving strategies. By regularly reviewing your progress and making necessary adjustments, you can ensure that your savings continue to grow and support your evolving financial needs.

Staying Motivated: Motivation is key to maintaining consistency in your saving efforts. One way to stay motivated is by setting up visual reminders of your financial goals, such as a vision board or a savings tracker. Seeing your progress can provide a sense of accomplishment and encourage you to keep going. Additionally, rewarding yourself for reaching milestones—whether it's hitting a savings target or successfully implementing a new saving strategy—can help reinforce positive behavior.

Automating and Simplifying: Automation is not just a convenience; it's a powerful tool for maintaining consistency. By automating your savings, you remove the need for constant decisionmaking and reduce the likelihood of forgetting or skipping contributions. Simplifying your financial processes—such as consolidating accounts or using financial apps to track spending—can also make it easier to stay on top of your savings plan.

The Role of Education and Continuous Learning

Financial education plays a crucial role in your ability to save effectively. Understanding the nuances of different saving strategies, interest rates, and financial products allows you to make informed decisions that maximize your savings potential.

Continual Learning: The financial landscape is constantly evolving, with new products, technologies, and strategies emerging all the time. Staying informed about these changes can help you adapt your saving strategies and take advantage of new opportunities. Reading financial books, following reputable financial blogs, and attending seminars or workshops are all excellent ways to deepen your knowledge and stay ahead of the curve.

Seeking Professional Advice: While selfeducation is important, there are times when seeking advice from a financial professional can be invaluable. A financial advisor can provide personalized guidance tailored to your specific goals and circumstances. Whether you're navigating complex savings strategies, planning for retirement, or considering major financial decisions, professional advice can help you avoid costly mistakes and optimize your savings plan.

The LongTerm Benefits of Mastering Saving

Mastering the art of saving offers benefits that extend far beyond simply having more money in the bank. By saving consistently and effectively, you gain financial security, reduce stress, and create opportunities for future growth.

Financial Security: One of the most significant benefits of a strong savings habit is the sense of security it provides. Having a well funded emergency fund, sufficient savings for future goals, and a buffer against unexpected expenses gives you peace of mind and reduces the financial anxiety that many people experience. This security allows you to make decisions based on what's best for your long term wellbeing, rather than reacting out of fear or necessity.

Greater Opportunities: Saving effectively opens up a world of opportunities. With a solid financial foundation, you have the freedom to pursue your passions, invest in new ventures, or take calculated risks that can lead to greater rewards. Whether it's starting a business, traveling the world, or pursuing further education, having the financial resources to support your dreams is a powerful enabler of personal and professional growth.

Wealth Building: Consistent saving is the cornerstone of wealth building. By saving regularly and allowing your money to grow through compound interest and strategic investments, you can accumulate wealth over time. This wealth not only supports your current lifestyle but also provides for future generations, helping you leave a lasting legacy.

Chapter 5

Investing for the Future

Investing is a critical component of the financial freedom formula. While saving lays the foundation for financial security, investing is what builds wealth and propels you toward longterm financial goals. By putting your money to work in various assets, you can grow your wealth, hedge against inflation, and secure your financial future. In this chapter, we'll delve into the basics of investing, the importance of diversification, stock market strategies, and the benefits of real estate investment.

Investment Basics

Before diving into specific investment strategies, it's essential to understand the basic principles of investing. At its core, investing involves allocating money with the expectation of generating a return or profit over time. However, with potential rewards come risks, and understanding these risks is crucial to making informed investment decisions.

Understanding Different Asset Classes: An asset class is a category of investments that exhibit similar characteristics and behavior in the marketplace. The main asset classes include stocks, bonds, real estate, commodities, and cash equivalents. Each asset class has its own risk and return profile, making them suitable for different types of investors and financial goals.

Stocks: When you buy stocks, you are purchasing a share of ownership in a company. Stocks have historically offered high potential returns, but they also come with higher volatility and risk, especially in the short term.

Bonds: Bonds are essentially loans that investors make to corporations or governments. In return, the issuer pays interest at regular intervals and returns the principal at maturity. Bonds are generally considered safer than stocks, but they also offer lower returns.

Real Estate: Investing in real estate involves buying property with the intention of generating income (through rent) or appreciation in value. Real estate can offer steady cash flow and long term growth, but it requires significant upfront capital and ongoing management.

Commodities: Commodities include physical assets like gold, oil, and agricultural products. They can be used as a hedge against inflation or economic instability but can be volatile and are influenced by supply and demand dynamics.

Cash Equivalents: These include short term, low risk investments like savings accounts, money market funds, and Treasury bills. While they provide stability, they typically offer the lowest returns, often not enough to outpace inflation.

Risk vs. Reward: How to Assess Investments: Every investment carries some level of risk, which is the possibility of losing money or earning less than expected. Generally, the potential for higher returns comes with higher risk. Understanding your risk tolerance—how much risk you're willing and able to take—is crucial in choosing the right investments.

Risk Tolerance: Your risk tolerance is influenced by factors such as your financial goals, investment horizon, income, and personal comfort with uncertainty. For example, younger investors with a long time horizon might be more willing to take on higherrisk investments, like stocks, because they have time to recover from market downturns. On the other hand, someone nearing retirement may prefer more conservative investments, like bonds, to preserve capital.

Return on Investment (ROI): ROI is a measure of the profitability of an investment. It's calculated by dividing the net profit by the initial investment cost. When assessing investments, it's important to compare the potential ROI against the risk you're taking on. This helps ensure that you're being adequately compensated for the risks involved.

Volatility: Volatility refers to the degree of variation in an asset's price over time. High volatility means that the asset's price can change dramatically in a short period, which can be both an opportunity and a risk. Understanding the volatility of an investment helps you manage expectations and assess whether it fits your risk tolerance.

The Importance of Diversification

Diversification is one of the most fundamental principles of investing. It involves spreading your investments across different asset classes, industries, and geographic regions to reduce risk. The idea is that by holding a variety of assets, the poor performance of one investment can be offset by better performance in another, leading to more stable overall returns.

Why Diversification Matters: No investment is without risk, and the market is inherently unpredictable. Diversification helps protect your portfolio from the impact of market volatility. For example, if you invest only in tech stocks and the technology sector experiences a downturn, your entire portfolio could suffer. However, if you also have investments in bonds, real estate, or other sectors, the losses in tech stocks may be cushioned by gains elsewhere.

How to Diversify Your Portfolio: Diversification can be achieved in several ways:

Across Asset Classes: This involves investing in a mix of stocks, bonds, real estate, and other assets. Each asset class responds differently to market conditions, providing a balance between risk and return.

Within Asset Classes: Even within a single asset class, diversification is important. For example, within your stock portfolio, you can diversify by investing in companies from different sectors (e.g., healthcare, technology, consumer goods) and regions (e.g., domestic vs. international stocks).

Through Investment Funds: Mutual funds and exchange traded funds (ETFs) are popular tools for diversification. These funds pool money from many investors to purchase a diversified portfolio of stocks, bonds, or other assets. This allows individual investors to gain exposure to a broad range of assets with a single investment.

The Role of Rebalancing: Over time, the performance of different investments will cause your portfolio's asset allocation to drift from its original target. For example, if stocks perform well, they may end up constituting a larger percentage of your portfolio than intended, increasing your risk exposure. Rebalancing involves periodically adjusting your portfolio to maintain your desired level of risk and diversification.

Stock Market Strategies

Investing in the stock market is one of the most common ways to grow wealth over time. However, it requires a solid understanding of the market, careful planning, and disciplined execution.

Introduction to Stock Market Investing: The stock market is a marketplace where shares of publicly traded companies are bought and sold. Investors purchase stocks with the expectation that the company will grow and increase in value, leading to a rise in the stock price. Stocks can be traded on major exchanges like the New York Stock Exchange (NYSE) or Nasdaq, or over the counter for smaller or less liquid companies.

Common Stocks vs. Preferred Stocks: Common stocks represent ownership in a company and typically come with voting rights, allowing shareholders to influence corporate decisions. Preferred stocks, on the other hand, do not usually have voting rights but offer fixed dividends and have priority over common stocks in the event of liquidation.

Growth Stocks vs. Value Stocks: Growth stocks are shares of companies expected to grow at an aboveaverage rate compared to the market. These companies typically reinvest profits to fuel growth rather than pay dividends. Value stocks, by contrast, are shares of companies that are considered undervalued by the market. They often pay dividends and may be less volatile than growth stocks.

Building a Stock Portfolio: A well constructed stock portfolio aligns with your investment goals, risk tolerance, and time horizon. Here are some key steps to building a stock portfolio:

Determine Your Investment Strategy: Decide whether you want to focus on growth, income, or a balanced approach. Your strategy will influence the types of stocks you choose and how you allocate your investments.

Select Individual Stocks or Funds: If you have the time and expertise, you may choose to invest in individual stocks. However, if you prefer a more hands off approach or want instant diversification, investing in mutual funds or ETFs that track an index (like the S&P 500) might be a better option.

Consider Sector Allocation: To diversify within your stock portfolio, consider allocating funds to different sectors of the economy, such as technology, healthcare, finance, and consumer goods. This reduces the risk that poor performance in one sector will significantly impact your overall portfolio.

Invest Regularly: One of the best ways to build a strong portfolio is to invest regularly, regardless of market conditions. This approach, known as dollar cost averaging, involves investing a fixed amount of money at regular intervals, which can help mitigate the impact of market volatility.

Dollar-Cost Averaging: Dollar Cost averaging (DCA) is a strategy where you invest a fixed amount of money into an investment at regular intervals, regardless of the asset's price. This approach reduces the risk of making large investments at an inopportune time, such as when the market is at a peak.

How DCA Works: When prices are high, your fixed investment amount buys fewer shares, and when prices are low, it buys more shares. Over time, this strategy can lower the average cost per share compared to investing a lump sum at one time. DCA is particularly effective in volatile markets, where prices can fluctuate significantly over short periods.

Benefits of DCA: Dollar Cost averaging can help take the emotion out of investing, as it encourages discipline and reduces the temptation to time the market. It also allows you to benefit from market downturns by buying more shares when prices are low, potentially increasing your returns in the long run.

Real Estate Investment

Real estate has long been a popular investment choice due to its potential for steady income, long term appreciation, and diversification benefits. While real estate requires more hands on management than stocks or bonds, it can be a powerful tool for building wealth.

Buying Property for Investment: Investing in real estate typically involves purchasing property with the intention of generating rental income or selling it for a profit in the future. There are several types of real estate investments, including residential properties (single family homes, apartments), commercial properties (office buildings, retail spaces), and land.

Evaluating Investment Properties: When buying property for investment, it's crucial to evaluate the potential profitability and risks involved. Here are key factors to consider when evaluating an investment property:

Location: The location of a property is one of the most critical factors in determining its value and potential for appreciation. Properties in areas with strong job markets, good schools, and access to amenities typically appreciate more over time and attract higher quality tenants.

Cash Flow: Cash flow is the difference between the income generated by the property (primarily through rent) and the expenses associated with owning it, such as mortgage payments, property taxes, insurance, maintenance, and management fees. Positive cash flow means that the property generates more income than it costs to maintain, making it a viable long term investment.

Property Condition: The condition of the property affects both its purchase price and ongoing maintenance costs. A property that needs significant repairs might be purchased at a discount, but the cost of renovations could reduce profitability. It's important to conduct thorough inspections and estimate the costs of repairs and upgrades before purchasing.

Market Trends: Understanding the local real estate market is essential for making informed decisions. Look at trends in property values, rental rates, and occupancy levels in the area. Research whether the market is appreciating, stable, or declining, as this will impact both the potential for capital appreciation and rental income.

Real Estate vs. Stocks: Which is better? Deciding between real estate and stocks as your primary investment vehicle depends on your financial goals, risk tolerance, and preferences. Both asset classes have their advantages and drawbacks:

Liquidity: Stocks are highly liquid, meaning they can be bought and sold quickly with minimal transaction costs. Real estate, on the other hand, is relatively illiquid. Selling a property can take time, and transaction costs (like agent fees, closing costs, and taxes) can be substantial.

Volatility: The stock market is more volatile than real estate, with prices fluctuating frequently due to economic, political, and company specific factors. Real estate tends to be more stable, with property values generally increasing steadily over time, although it can be subject to market downturns, as seen during the housing crash of 2008.

Income Generation: Real estate can provide a steady stream of income through rental payments, which can be particularly attractive for investors seeking cash flow. While some stocks offer dividends, these are typically smaller and less predictable than rental income.

Capital Requirements: Investing in real estate usually requires significant upfront capital, not only for the purchase price but also for ongoing expenses such as property management, maintenance, and insurance. In contrast, you can start investing in stocks with relatively small amounts of money, and there are no ongoing costs other than trading fees and taxes.

Diversification: Stocks allow for easy diversification across industries and geographies, which helps manage risk. Diversifying within real estate is more challenging, as each property requires a substantial investment. However, real estate investment trusts (REITs) offer a way to gain exposure to real estate while still enjoying the benefits of diversification.

Leverage: Real estate allows for the use of leverage, meaning you can borrow money (usually through a mortgage) to finance the purchase of a property. This can amplify your returns if the property appreciates, but it also increases risk, as you must make mortgage payments regardless of whether the property generates income.

The Benefits of Rental Income: Rental income is one of the most attractive aspects of real estate investing. It provides a regular, passive income stream that can supplement your other sources of income and contribute to financial independence.

Steady Cash Flow: One of the primary benefits of rental income is the steady cash flow it can provide. As long as the property is occupied and well maintained, you can expect to receive regular rent payments. This cash flow can be used to cover the property's expenses, pay down the mortgage, or reinvest in other opportunities.

Inflation Hedge: Real estate tends to appreciate over time, often at a rate that outpaces inflation. Additionally, rental income typically increases with inflation, as landlords can raise rents in response to rising costs of living. This makes rental properties a good hedge against inflation, preserving the purchasing power of your income and assets.

Tax Advantages: Real estate investors benefit from several tax advantages, including deductions for mortgage interest, property taxes, depreciation, and certain operating expenses. These deductions can significantly reduce your taxable income, increasing the overall return on your investment.

Wealth Building Through Equity: As you pay down the mortgage on a rental property, you build equity—the portion of the property you own outright. Over time, this equity can grow as the property appreciates in value, contributing to your net worth. You can also leverage this equity to finance additional investments or improve your cash flow.

Potential for Appreciation: While rental income provides immediate cash flow, real estate also offers the potential for long term appreciation. If the property increases in value, you can sell it at a profit or continue to benefit from higher rental income. However, real estate markets can be cyclical, so it's important to consider the timing of your purchase and sale.

Control Over Investment: Unlike stocks or bonds, where you have little control over the performance of the underlying company, real estate allows you to directly influence the success of your investment. You can make improvements to the property, choose tenants, and set rental rates, all of which can enhance your returns.

Chapter 6

Protecting Your Wealth

Achieving financial freedom isn't just about accumulating wealth—it's equally important to protect what you've built. Without proper safeguards, your financial assets could be eroded by unexpected events, legal challenges, or inefficient wealth transfer strategies. Protecting your wealth involves a comprehensive approach that includes insurance, estate planning, and strategies to minimize taxes on your estate. In this chapter, we'll explore these critical aspects of wealth protection.

1. Insurance Essentials

Insurance is a fundamental tool in safeguarding your wealth against unforeseen risks. While many people think of insurance as just another expense, it's actually a crucial part of any financial plan, providing a safety net that can protect your assets and secure your financial future.

Types of Insurance You Need: There are various types of insurance, each designed to protect different aspects of your life and wealth. Depending on your circumstances, you may need one or more of the following:

Health Insurance: Health insurance is essential for covering medical expenses, which can be incredibly high without coverage. A serious illness or accident could wipe out your savings if you're uninsured. Health insurance helps protect you from these potentially devastating costs.

Life Insurance: Life insurance provides financial protection to your loved ones in the event of your death. There are two main types of life insurance: term life insurance, which provides coverage for a specific period, and whole life insurance, which offers lifelong coverage and includes a savings component. Life insurance can help cover funeral costs, pay off debts, and provide income replacement for your dependents.

Disability Insurance: Disability insurance replaces a portion of your income if you're unable to work due to illness or injury. Given that the risk of becoming disabled during your working years is higher than many people realize, disability insurance is a vital form of protection, especially for those who rely on their income to meet financial obligations.

Homeowners or Renters Insurance: Homeowners insurance protects your home and its contents against damage or loss from events like fire, theft, or natural disasters. Renters insurance provides similar protection for those who rent their homes, covering personal belongings and liability.

Auto Insurance: Auto insurance is mandatory in most places and covers damages and liabilities resulting from car accidents. Without adequate auto insurance, you could be financially responsible for repairs, medical bills, and legal fees resulting from an accident.

Liability Insurance: Liability insurance protects you from financial losses if you are sued for causing injury or property damage to someone else. This type of insurance is often included in homeowners or auto policies but can also be purchased as a separate umbrella policy for additional coverage.

Long Term Care Insurance: Long Term care insurance helps cover the costs of care if you develop a chronic illness or disability that requires assistance with daily activities. With the rising costs of healthcare and longer life expectancies, long term care insurance can protect your savings from being depleted by expensive long term care needs.

How to Choose the Right Insurance Policies: Selecting the right insurance policies involves assessing your specific needs, evaluating potential risks, and comparing different options to find the most suitable coverage.

Assessing Your Needs: Start by identifying the areas of your life that need protection. Consider factors like your age, health, family situation, income, assets, and liabilities. For example, a young, single professional may prioritize disability and auto insurance, while a family breadwinner might focus on life and health insurance.

Evaluating Potential Risks: Consider the likelihood and potential impact of various risks. For instance, if you live in an area prone to natural disasters, homeowners insurance with adequate coverage for those events is crucial. Similarly, if you have dependents, life insurance becomes more important to ensure their financial security.

Comparing Coverage Options: Once you've identified your insurance needs, compare different policies from multiple insurers. Pay attention to coverage limits, exclusions, deductibles, and premiums. It's also essential to consider the insurer's reputation, customer service, and claims process.

Balancing Cost and Coverage: While it's tempting to choose the cheapest policy, it's important to strike a balance between cost and coverage. Inadequate coverage could leave you vulnerable to significant financial losses, so ensure that the policy you choose provides sufficient protection for your needs.

Insurance as a Wealth Protection Tool: Insurance not only helps cover the costs of unexpected events but also plays a critical role in preserving your wealth by preventing financial setbacks. Here's how insurance functions as a tool for wealth protection:

Preserving Assets: By transferring the financial risk of significant losses to an insurance company, you can protect your savings and investments from being depleted by medical bills, lawsuits, or property damage. For example, if your home is destroyed in a fire, homeowners insurance can cover the rebuilding costs, saving you from a major financial hit.

Providing Peace of Mind: Knowing that you have adequate insurance coverage allows you to focus on other financial goals without the constant worry of potential losses. This peace of mind is a valuable aspect of wealth protection, enabling you to make long term financial decisions with confidence.

Supporting Estate Planning: Life insurance can be an integral part of your estate plan, providing liquidity to cover estate taxes, pay off debts, or equalize inheritances among beneficiaries. Additionally, some insurance policies, like whole life or universal life insurance, accumulate cash value over time, which can be borrowed against or used to supplement retirement income.

Ensuring Business Continuity: If you own a business, insurance can protect against risks that could jeopardize your business's survival, such as the loss of a key employee or damage to your property. Business interruption insurance, key person insurance, and liability insurance are essential for maintaining the financial health of your business.

2. Estate Planning and Wealth Transfer

Estate planning is the process of arranging for the management and distribution of your assets after your death. A well structured estate plan ensures that your wealth is transferred according to your wishes while minimizing taxes and legal complications. It's an essential component of protecting your wealth and providing for your loved ones.

The Basics of Estate Planning: Estate planning involves several key elements, each serving a specific purpose in managing and transferring your assets:

Wills: A will is a legal document that outlines how you want your assets distributed after your death. It also allows you to name an executor, who is responsible for managing your estate, and a guardian for any minor children. Without a will, your assets will be distributed according to state laws, which may not align with your wishes.

Trusts: A trust is a legal entity that holds assets on behalf of beneficiaries. Trusts can be used to manage and protect assets during your lifetime and ensure a smooth transfer of wealth after your death. There are several types of trusts, including revocable living trusts, irrevocable trusts, and special needs trusts, each serving different purposes.

Powers of Attorney: A power of attorney (POA) is a legal document that grants someone the authority to act on your behalf if you become incapacitated. There are two main types of POAs: a durable power of attorney for financial matters and a healthcare power of attorney for medical decisions.

Beneficiary Designations: Many assets, such as life insurance policies, retirement accounts, and payableondeath bank accounts, allow you to designate beneficiaries. These assets typically bypass probate and go directly to the named beneficiaries upon your death.

Advance Directives: Advance directives, such as a living will or health care proxy, provide instructions for your medical care if you are unable to communicate your wishes. These documents can help ensure that your healthcare preferences are honored and reduce the burden on your family during difficult times.

Wills, Trusts, and Inheritance: Understanding the role of wills, trusts, and inheritance in estate planning is crucial for protecting your wealth and ensuring that it's distributed according to your wishes.

Wills: A will is the cornerstone of any estate plan. It allows you to specify who receives your assets, how they are distributed, and who will be responsible for carrying out your wishes. Without a will, the state will determine how your assets are divided, which could lead to disputes among heirs and unintended consequences.

Trusts: Trusts offer more flexibility and control over how your assets are managed and distributed. For example, a revocable living trust allows you to retain control of your assets during your lifetime and designate how they should be distributed after your death. Trusts can also provide protection from creditors, reduce estate taxes, and avoid probate, which is the legal process of administering a deceased person's estate.

Inheritance: Planning for the inheritance of your assets involves more than just deciding who gets what. It's important to consider the tax implications, potential conflicts among heirs, and the impact of your decisions on family dynamics. Clear communication and careful planning can help prevent disputes and ensure that your wishes are carried out smoothly.

Minimizing Taxes on Your Estate: One of the primary goals of estate planning is to minimize the tax burden on your estate, allowing more of your wealth to be passed on to your heirs. Here are some strategies to reduce estate taxes:

Gift Tax Exemptions: The IRS allows you to give away a certain amount of money or property each year without incurring gift taxes. As of 2024, the annual gift tax exclusion is $17,000 per recipient. Making regular gifts during your lifetime can reduce the size of your estate and, therefore, the estate taxes owed.

Lifetime Gift Tax Exemption: In addition to the annual exclusion, you have a lifetime gift tax exemption, which is the amount you can give away without paying gift taxes. As of 2024, the lifetime exemption is $12.92 million. By strategically using your lifetime gift tax exemption, you can transfer substantial wealth to your heirs during your lifetime, reducing the value of your estate and the taxes that may be due upon your death.

Establishing Trusts: Trusts can be powerful tools for minimizing estate taxes. For instance, an irrevocable life insurance trust (ILIT) removes the death benefit of a life insurance policy from your taxable estate. Similarly, a charitable remainder trust allows you to donate assets to a charity while retaining income from those assets during your lifetime, with the remainder going to the charity upon your death. These types of trusts can help reduce your estate's taxable value while supporting charitable causes or providing for your heirs.

Qualified Personal Residence Trusts (QPRTs): A QPRT allows you to transfer ownership of your primary or secondary residence to a trust while retaining the right to live in the home for a set number of years. After the term ends, the property passes to your beneficiaries at a reduced gift tax value, which can significantly lower the taxable value of the property within your estate.

GenerationSkipping Transfer (GST) Tax Exemption: The GST tax applies to transfers of wealth to grandchildren or other individuals who are more than one generation younger than you. However, each taxpayer is granted a GST tax exemption, which allows you to transfer a certain amount of assets to these younger beneficiaries without incurring GST taxes. Leveraging this exemption can be an effective way to preserve wealth across generations.

Charitable Giving: Making charitable donations can reduce your estate tax liability while supporting causes you care about. Charitable contributions are generally deductible from your taxable estate, and setting up a charitable trust or foundation can further optimize your tax benefits.

Family Limited Partnerships (FLPs): An FLP allows you to transfer business interests or other assets to family members while retaining control over the assets. By gifting partnership interests to your heirs, you can reduce the value of your taxable estate and apply valuation discounts for lack of marketability and control, further reducing estate and gift taxes.

Portability of the Estate Tax Exemption: Under current tax laws, married couples can take advantage of the portability of the estate tax exemption. If one spouse dies and does not use up their full exemption, the surviving spouse can add the unused portion to their own exemption, effectively doubling the amount that can be passed on to heirs without incurring estate taxes. To benefit from this, the surviving spouse must file an estate tax return, even if no taxes are owed at the time of the first spouse's death.

Regularly Reviewing Your Estate Plan: Tax laws and your personal circumstances can change over time, so it's important to regularly review and update your estate plan. This ensures that your plan remains aligned with your current goals and takes advantage of any new opportunities to minimize taxes. Working with an estate planning attorney and financial advisor can help you stay informed about changes in tax laws and how they might impact your estate.

Chapter 7

Achieving Financial Independence

Achieving financial independence is the ultimate goal for many who seek to escape the constraints of traditional employment and enjoy a life of freedom and choice. Financial independence means having enough wealth and income generating assets to cover your living expenses indefinitely, allowing you to retire early or pursue other passions without financial stress. This chapter explores the concepts, strategies, and mindsets essential to achieving and sustaining financial independence, with a particular focus on the Financial Independence, Retire Early (FIRE) movement and the importance of maintaining your newfound freedom.

1. Financial Independence, Retire Early (FIRE)

The FIRE movement has gained significant popularity over the past decade, attracting a growing number of individuals who seek to break free from the conventional worklife paradigm. At its core, FIRE is about saving and investing aggressively to reach a level of financial independence that allows for early retirement. While the idea of retiring in your 30s or 40s may seem radical to some, it's a feasible goal for those who are disciplined, strategic, and committed to living below their means.

Understanding the FIRE Movement: The FIRE movement is rooted in the principles of financial independence and frugality. It encourages individuals to save a substantial portion of their income, often 50% or more, and invest those savings in assets that will grow over time. The goal is to accumulate enough wealth so that you can live off the returns of your investments, effectively making work optional.

Origins and Philosophy: The FIRE movement draws inspiration from the book Your Money or Your Life by Joe Dominguez and Vicki Robin, which emphasizes the relationship between time, money, and life energy. The philosophy behind FIRE is that by carefully managing your money and focusing on what truly brings you joy, you can reduce your dependence on a traditional job and reclaim your time. The movement challenges the societal norm of working until your 60s or 70s and instead advocates for a life of financial autonomy.

Types of FIRE: Within the FIRE movement, there are several variations that cater to different lifestyles and goals:

Lean FIRE: This approach involves achieving financial independence on a relatively modest budget. Individuals pursuing LeanFIRE typically live frugally and require a smaller nest egg to sustain their lifestyle. This might involve living in a low cost area, cutting unnecessary expenses, and embracing minimalism.

Fat FIRE: On the opposite end of the spectrum, Fat FIRE is for those who want to maintain or even enhance their standard of living in retirement. This approach requires a larger portfolio, as the goal is to have enough wealth to support a more comfortable or luxurious lifestyle without worrying about money.

Barista FIRE: Barista FIRE refers to individuals who achieve partial financial independence and choose to work part time or in less stressful jobs to cover some of their living expenses.

This allows them to enjoy more freedom and flexibility while still having a safety net of investments and savings.

Coast FIRE: Coast FIRE is a strategy where individuals save and invest aggressively in their early years, reaching a point where they no longer need to contribute to their retirement accounts. The idea is that their existing investments will grow enough over time to fund their retirement, allowing them to "coast" through their later working years without the pressure to save more.

Strategies for Early Retirement: Achieving early retirement through

FIRE requires a combination of high savings rates, smart investing, and lifestyle choices that align with your financial goals. Here are some key strategies to consider:

Aggressive Saving and Budgeting: The foundation of any FIRE plan is an aggressive savings rate. Many FIRE enthusiasts aim to save at least 50% of their income, with some pushing it even higher. To achieve this, you'll need to create a detailed budget, cut unnecessary expenses, and prioritize saving over spending. This might mean downsizing your home, driving a more affordable car, or forgoing expensive vacations in favor of more economical alternatives.

Investing for Growth: Saving alone isn't enough to achieve FIRE; you need to invest your savings in assets that will grow over time. The stock market is a popular choice for FIRE adherents due to its historical returns, but other options include real estate, bonds, and even alternative investments like peer to peer lending. The key is to choose a diversified portfolio that balances risk and reward while aligning with your time horizon and risk tolerance.

Minimizing Taxes: Taxes can eat into your investment returns, so it's important to take advantage of taxadvantaged accounts like 401(k)s, IRAs, and HSAs. These accounts offer significant tax benefits, either by allowing your money to grow taxfree or by reducing your taxable income. Additionally, strategies like tax loss harvesting, which involves selling investments at a loss to offset gains, can help minimize your tax burden.

Reducing Housing Costs: Housing is often the largest expense for most people, so finding ways to reduce this cost can accelerate your path to FIRE. Consider downsizing to a smaller home, moving to a more affordable location, or even house hacking—buying a property with multiple units and renting out the others to cover your mortgage. By reducing your housing costs, you can free up more money to invest and save.

Embracing Frugality and Minimalism: Frugality and minimalism are central to the FIRE philosophy. By focusing on what truly adds value to your life and cutting out unnecessary expenses, you can save more and reach financial independence sooner. This doesn't mean depriving yourself of enjoyment; rather, it's about making intentional choices that align with your long term goals.

Side Hustles and Additional Income Streams: In addition to saving more from your primary income, consider developing side hustles or additional income streams. Whether it's freelancing, investing in rental properties, or starting a small business, these extra sources of income can significantly boost your savings rate and help you reach FIRE faster.

The 4% Rule and Safe Withdrawal Rates: The 4% rule is a commonly cited guideline within the FIRE community for determining how much you can safely withdraw from your retirement savings each year without running out of money. It's based on the idea that if you withdraw 4% of your portfolio in the first year of retirement and adjust for inflation each subsequent year, your savings should last for at least 30 years.

Origins of the 4% Rule: The 4% rule was popularized by the "Trinity Study," a 1998 paper by three professors from Trinity University. The study analyzed historical data on stock and bond returns to determine the likelihood of a retirement portfolio lasting 30 years at different withdrawal rates. They found that a 4% initial withdrawal rate, with subsequent adjustments for inflation, was generally safe for a balanced portfolio of stocks and bonds.

Applying the 4% Rule: To use the 4% rule, start by calculating your annual living expenses. Then, multiply that number by 25 to determine the size of the portfolio you'll need to support those expenses in retirement. For example, if you need $40,000 per year to live comfortably, you would aim to accumulate a portfolio of $1 million ($40,000 x 25).

Limitations and Considerations: While the 4% rule is a helpful guideline, it's not without limitations. Market conditions, life expectancy, and unforeseen expenses can all impact the sustainability of your withdrawals. Some experts suggest using a more conservative withdrawal rate, such as 3.5%, to provide an additional cushion. Others recommend being flexible with your withdrawals, adjusting your spending in response to market performance.

Safe Withdrawal Rates and Longevity: Longevity is a significant factor in determining a safe withdrawal rate. As people live longer, the risk of outliving your savings increases. To mitigate this risk, consider strategies like delaying Social Security benefits to increase your guaranteed income, diversifying your income sources, or purchasing an annuity that provides lifetime income.

2. Sustaining Financial Freedom

Achieving financial independence is an incredible milestone, but maintaining it requires discipline, vigilance, and a commitment to your financial goals. It's easy to let your guard down after reaching FIRE, but staying on track is essential to ensuring that your wealth lasts and that you continue to live the life you envisioned.

Avoiding Lifestyle Inflation: One of the biggest threats to sustaining financial freedom is lifestyle inflation—when your spending increases in proportion to your income or wealth. After reaching FIRE, you may be tempted to upgrade your lifestyle, whether it's buying a larger home, splurging on luxury items, or taking more extravagant vacations. However, these increased expenses can quickly erode your financial security.

Recognizing the Signs of Lifestyle Inflation: Lifestyle inflation often creeps in gradually, making it difficult to notice. It can start with small, seemingly insignificant upgrades that add up over time. For example, you might begin dining out more frequently, purchasing more expensive clothing, or upgrading your car. While these changes may not seem harmful on their own, they can collectively strain your budget and reduce the longevity of your investments.

Strategies to Combat Lifestyle Inflation: To avoid lifestyle inflation, focus on maintaining the frugality and discipline that helped you achieve financial independence in the first place. Set a budget that aligns with your long term goals and stick to it. Regularly review your expenses to identify areas where you might be overspending and make adjustments as needed. Additionally, keep your financial goals front and center, reminding yourself of the reasons you pursued FIRE and the freedom it provides.

Living Below Your Means: Even after achieving financial independence, it's wise to continue living below your means. This doesn't mean depriving yourself of enjoyment; rather, it's about making intentional spending choices that align with your values and financial goals. Living below your means provides a buffer against unexpected expenses, market downturns, and other financial challenges that may arise. It also allows you to continue growing your wealth, giving you greater flexibility and security in the long run.

Staying on Track with Your Financial Goals: Achieving financial independence doesn't mean your financial journey is over. It's important to regularly revisit and reassess your goals to ensure you stay on track. Your priorities, circumstances, and aspirations may evolve over time, so your financial plan should be flexible enough to accommodate these changes.

Regular Financial CheckIns: Schedule regular financial check-ins to review your budget, investments, and overall financial health. These check-ins can be quarterly or annually, depending on your preference. During these reviews, assess whether your spending aligns with your long term goals, evaluate the performance of your investments, and make any necessary adjustments to your plan.

Adapting to Life Changes: Life is unpredictable, and your financial plan should be adaptable to significant life changes such as marriage, the birth of a child, a career change, or a health crisis. These events may require you to adjust your spending, reassess your risk tolerance, or reevaluate your retirement timeline. By being proactive and flexible, you can navigate these changes without compromising your financial independence.

Continual Learning and Growth: Staying informed about personal finance, investing, and economic trends is essential for sustaining financial independence. Continue to educate yourself through books, podcasts, online courses, and other resources. Engaging with a community of like minded individuals who share your FIRE goals can also provide valuable insights, support, and motivation.

Reinvesting for Future Growth: Even after reaching financial independence, it's important to keep investing and growing your wealth. Reinvesting dividends, rental income, or other returns from your investments can help your portfolio continue to grow, providing additional security and enabling you to maintain or even enhance your lifestyle over time. This approach also ensures that you remain prepared for any future financial challenges.

Giving Back: Philanthropy and Legacy Building: Once you've achieved financial independence, you may feel a desire to give back and make a positive impact on the world. Philanthropy and legacy building can be meaningful ways to use your wealth for the greater good while also leaving a lasting legacy.

The Role of Philanthropy in Financial Independence: Philanthropy is not only about donating money but also about using your time, skills, and resources to support causes you care about. Giving back can provide a sense of purpose and fulfillment, especially after you've achieved financial independence. Whether it's supporting education, healthcare, the environment, or social justice, philanthropy allows you to contribute to something larger than yourself.

Strategic Giving: To maximize the impact of your philanthropic efforts, consider adopting a strategic approach to giving. This involves identifying causes that align with your values, setting clear goals for your contributions, and researching organizations to ensure your donations are used effectively. You might also consider setting up a donor advised fund (DAF), which allows you to donate assets, receive an immediate tax deduction, and recommend grants to charities over time.

Building a Legacy: Legacy building goes beyond financial independence; it's about creating something that will endure beyond your lifetime. This could involve establishing a charitable foundation, endowing scholarships, or leaving a significant bequest to a cause you're passionate about. Legacy planning also includes ensuring that your wealth is transferred to the next generation in a way that reflects your values and supports their financial security.

Involving Family in Philanthropy: Engaging your family in your philanthropic efforts can be a powerful way to pass on your values and instill a sense of responsibility in future generations. Involving your children or other heirs in your charitable giving decisions can help them develop their own philanthropic interests and understand the importance of giving back.

Balancing Philanthropy with Financial Security: While giving back is important, it's also essential to balance your philanthropic efforts with maintaining your own financial security. Ensure that your charitable contributions are sustainable and do not jeopardize your financial independence. This might involve setting a budget for your donations or creating a plan that allows you to give back while still preserving your wealth for your future needs and those of your family.

Chapter 8

Overcoming Obstacles

The journey to financial freedom is not always smooth. Along the way, you'll likely encounter various obstacles that challenge your resolve and test your commitment. These obstacles can come in many forms—financial setbacks, unexpected crises, or even psychological barriers that undermine your confidence and motivation. However, overcoming these obstacles is an integral part of achieving lasting financial independence. This chapter explores strategies for dealing with financial setbacks, rebuilding after a crisis, and maintaining the motivation needed to stay on track toward your financial goals.

1. Dealing with Financial Setbacks

Financial setbacks are inevitable. Whether it's an unexpected medical bill, a job loss, a failed investment, or a global economic downturn, setbacks can disrupt your financial plans and make it feel like you're back at square one. How you respond to these challenges can significantly impact your ability to recover and continue progressing toward financial freedom.

How to Recover from Financial Mistakes: Everyone makes financial mistakes at some point. These mistakes can range from overspending on credit to making a poor investment decision. The key to recovery is not to dwell on the mistake but to learn from it and take corrective action.

Acknowledge and Analyze the Mistake: The first step in recovering from a financial mistake is to acknowledge it without denial or rationalization. Take a moment to reflect on what led to the mistake. Was it due to a lack of knowledge, impulse spending, or failing to plan for the future? By analyzing the root cause, you can identify what went wrong and how to avoid similar mistakes in the future.

Create a Recovery Plan: Once you've identified the mistake, it's time to create a recovery plan. Start by assessing the extent of the damage. For instance, if you've accumulated credit card debt, calculate how much you owe, the interest rates, and your minimum monthly payments. Then, develop a plan to pay off the debt as quickly as possible, prioritizing high interest accounts first. If the mistake involves an investment, consider whether it's worth holding onto the asset or if it's better to cut your losses and reinvest in something more stable.

Rebuild Your Financial Safety Net: After a financial setback, it's crucial to rebuild your financial safety net to prevent future crises. This might involve rebuilding your emergency fund, paying down debt, or reassessing your insurance coverage. Having a solid safety net in place can help you weather future storms without derailing your financial goals.

Seek Professional Advice: If you're unsure how to recover from a financial mistake or feel overwhelmed by the situation, consider seeking advice from a financial advisor or counselor. A professional can provide guidance, help you create a realistic recovery plan, and offer support as you work through your challenges.

Rebuilding After a Financial Crisis: Financial crises can be particularly devastating, whether they're caused by personal circumstances like a job loss or medical emergency, or large scale events like an economic recession or natural disaster. Rebuilding after such a crisis requires resilience, determination, and a strategic approach.

Assess the Damage: The first step in rebuilding after a financial crisis is to assess the full extent of the damage. This includes taking stock of your current financial situation—your income, expenses, debts, and assets. Understanding where you stand financially will help you prioritize your actions and focus on the most critical areas first.

Prioritize Immediate Needs: During a financial crisis, it's essential to prioritize your immediate needs, such as housing, food, utilities, and healthcare. Ensure that these basic needs are met before addressing other financial obligations. If necessary, explore government assistance programs, community resources, or charitable organizations that can provide temporary relief.

Develop a LongTerm Recovery Plan: Once your immediate needs are secured, develop a long term recovery plan. This plan should include steps to restore your financial stability, such as finding new employment, reducing expenses, negotiating with creditors, or consolidating debt. It's important to set realistic goals and timelines, recognizing that recovery may take time.

Focus on Income Generation: Increasing your income is a critical component of rebuilding after a financial crisis. This might involve finding a new job, taking on part time work, or starting a side hustle. Consider exploring new career paths or acquiring additional skills that can enhance your employability and earning potential.

Cut Unnecessary Expenses: In the aftermath of a financial crisis, it's important to scrutinize your expenses and eliminate any that are not essential. This might mean canceling subscriptions, dining out less frequently, or downsizing your living arrangements. Every dollar saved can be redirected toward rebuilding your financial foundation.

Seek Financial Assistance: If your financial crisis is severe, don't hesitate to seek financial assistance. This could include applying for unemployment benefits, accessing retirement funds (with caution), or taking out a low interest loan to cover essential expenses. Be mindful of the long term implications of any financial assistance you receive, and avoid taking on more debt than you can manage.

Embrace Resilience and Adaptability: Rebuilding after a financial crisis requires resilience—the ability to bounce back from adversity—and adaptability—the willingness to change course when necessary. These qualities are essential for navigating the challenges of recovery and emerging stronger on the other side. Keep a positive attitude, stay focused on your goals, and be prepared to adjust your plans as circumstances change.

The Importance of Resilience and Adaptability: Resilience and adaptability are crucial traits for anyone on the path to financial freedom. Life is unpredictable, and the ability to persevere through setbacks and adapt to changing circumstances can make the difference between success and failure.

Building Resilience: Resilience is the mental and emotional strength that allows you to recover from difficulties. It involves maintaining a positive outlook, staying motivated, and refusing to give up, even in the face of adversity. To build resilience, focus on developing a growth mindset—believing that you can learn and improve from your experiences, no matter how challenging they may be. Surround yourself with supportive people, practice selfcare, and seek out resources that can help you navigate difficult times.

Cultivating Adaptability: Adaptability is the ability to adjust to new situations and change your approach when necessary. In the context of financial freedom, this might mean being open to new career opportunities, adjusting your financial goals in response to life changes, or exploring alternative investment strategies when market conditions shift. Cultivating adaptability involves staying flexible, being willing to learn, and embracing change as an opportunity for growth.

Learning from Setbacks: Every setback is an opportunity to learn and grow. Instead of viewing financial mistakes or crises as failures, see them as valuable lessons that can help you make better decisions in the future. Reflect on what you've learned, apply those lessons to your financial plan, and use them to build a stronger foundation for the future.

Maintaining a LongTerm Perspective: It's easy to get discouraged by short term setbacks, but maintaining a long term perspective can help you stay focused on your ultimate goals. Remember that the path to financial freedom is a marathon, not a sprint, and that setbacks are just temporary obstacles on the way to success. By keeping your eye on the bigger picture, you can maintain your motivation and resilience, even during challenging times.

2. Staying Motivated on the Path to Financial Freedom

Achieving financial freedom is a long term endeavor that requires sustained effort, discipline, and motivation. Along the way, it's natural to encounter periods of doubt, frustration, or even burnout. Staying motivated is essential for maintaining momentum and ensuring that you continue to make progress toward your financial goals.

Maintaining a Positive Financial Mindset: Your mindset plays a crucial role in your financial success. A positive financial mindset is one that embraces the possibilities of growth, focuses on solutions rather than problems, and maintains optimism in the face of challenges.

The Power of Positive Thinking: Positive thinking can have a profound impact on your financial journey. When you believe in your ability to achieve financial freedom, you're more likely to take the actions necessary to make it a reality. Conversely, negative thinking can lead to self doubt, procrastination, and a lack of motivation. To cultivate a positive financial mindset, practice gratitude for what you already have, focus on your strengths, and visualize the life you want to create.

Affirmations and Visualization: Affirmations are positive statements that reinforce your beliefs and intentions. By repeating affirmations related to financial success, you can reinforce your commitment to your goals and boost your confidence. Visualization is another powerful tool that involves imagining yourself achieving your financial goals in vivid detail. This mental rehearsal can help you stay motivated and focused on your desired outcome.

Overcoming Negative Self-Talk: Negative self talk can sabotage your progress by undermining your confidence and causing you to doubt your abilities. It's important to recognize and challenge these negative thoughts when they arise. Replace self defeating thoughts with positive affirmations, remind yourself of your past successes, and focus on the progress you've already made.

Practicing Financial Mindfulness: Financial mindfulness involves being present and aware of your financial decisions and their impact on your overall goals. By practicing mindfulness, you can make more intentional choices, avoid impulsive spending, and stay aligned with your long term objectives. Techniques such as meditation, journaling, or simply taking a few moments each day to reflect on your financial goals can help you maintain a positive and focused mindset.

The Role of Accountability: Accountability is a powerful motivator that can help you stay on track and committed to your financial goals. When you hold yourself accountable—or enlist the help of others to do so—you're more likely to follow through on your plans and make consistent progress.

Accountability Partners: An accountability partner is someone who shares your financial goals and supports you in achieving your objectives. This could be a friend, family member, or colleague who is also on a journey toward financial freedom. The role of an accountability partner is to provide encouragement, share insights, and hold you accountable for the commitments you make. Regular check-ins with your accountability partner can help keep you focused, motivated, and on track.

Financial Accountability Groups: Joining a financial accountability group can also be an effective way to stay motivated. These groups, whether online or in person, bring together individuals who are working toward similar financial goals. In a group setting, members share their progress, discuss challenges, and provide mutual support. The collective wisdom of the group can offer new perspectives, practical tips, and a sense of community that can be invaluable on your journey.

Tracking Your Progress: One of the most effective ways to maintain accountability is by tracking your progress regularly. This can be done through budgeting apps, spreadsheets, or even a financial journal. By monitoring your income, expenses, savings, and investments, you can see how far you've come and identify areas where you might need to adjust your approach. Seeing tangible progress can boost your motivation and reinforce your commitment to your financial goals.

Setting Consequences and Rewards: Another way to stay accountable is by setting up consequences for not meeting your financial goals and rewards for achieving them. For example, you might set a goal to save a certain amount each month, with a small reward if you meet the target, such as treating yourself to something you enjoy. Conversely, if you don't meet the goal, you might impose a consequence, like skipping a luxury or leisure activity. These incentives can help you stay disciplined and motivated.

Celebrating Milestones and Small Wins: The journey to financial freedom is a long one, and it's important to recognize and celebrate your progress along the way. Celebrating milestones and small wins can provide the positive reinforcement needed to keep going, especially during challenging times.

Identifying Milestones: Milestones are significant achievements that represent progress toward your financial goals. These might include paying off a credit card, reaching a savings target, or investing in your first stock. Identifying these milestones in advance gives you something to look forward to and provides a sense of accomplishment when you reach them.

Celebrating Your Achievements: When you reach a milestone, take the time to celebrate your achievement. The celebration doesn't have to be extravagant—what matters is that you acknowledge the hard work and discipline that went into reaching your goal. Whether it's treating yourself to a nice meal, taking a day off to relax, or sharing your success with loved ones, celebrating reinforces the positive behaviors that led to the achievement.

Using Milestones to Build Momentum: Celebrating small wins helps to build momentum, making it easier to stay motivated and continue working toward your larger goals. Each milestone achieved reinforces the belief that financial freedom is possible, providing the encouragement needed to tackle the next challenge. By breaking down your financial journey into smaller, manageable steps, you can maintain a steady pace and keep your motivation high.

Reflecting on Your Journey: Periodically reflecting on your financial journey can also help maintain motivation. Take time to look back at where you started, the obstacles you've overcome, and the progress you've made. This reflection can give you a renewed sense of purpose and remind you of the reasons why you embarked on the path to financial freedom in the first place.

Conclusion

Overcoming obstacles is an inevitable part of the journey to financial freedom. Whether you're dealing with financial setbacks, navigating a crisis, or simply trying to stay motivated over the long term, the strategies outlined in this chapter can help you stay resilient, adaptable, and focused on your goals.

Dealing with financial setbacks requires a proactive approach—acknowledging mistakes, creating a recovery plan, and rebuilding your financial safety net. Resilience and adaptability are key qualities that will help you navigate the ups and downs of your financial journey, ensuring that you can bounce back from challenges and continue moving forward.

Staying motivated on the path to financial freedom is equally important. Maintaining a positive financial mindset, leveraging accountability, and celebrating milestones and small wins are all effective strategies for keeping your motivation high and your goals within reach. By staying focused, disciplined, and committed to your vision, you can overcome any obstacle and achieve the financial freedom you desire.

Remember, the journey to financial freedom is a marathon, not a sprint. It's about making consistent, intentional choices every day that align with your long-term goals. As you continue on this journey, know that each challenge you overcome and each milestone you achieve brings you one step closer to the financial independence and peace of mind you seek.

www.ingramcontent.com/pod-product-compliance
Lightning Source LLC
Chambersburg PA
CBHW052142220526
45471CB00004B/1489